BRASS

BUTTONS

and

SILVER

HORSESHOES

BRASS
BUTTONS
and
SILVER
HORSESHOES

STORIES FROM CANADA'S BRITISH WAR BRIDES

LINDA GRANFIELD

With the co-operation of Pier 21 Society

M&S

for Marion and Michael Seary,
who share their affections
– and their love of the sea

National Library of Canada Cataloguing in Publication Data

Granfield, Linda
    Brass buttons and silver horseshoes : stories from Canada's British war brides

ISBN 0-7710-3536-5 (bound). – ISBN 0-7710-3535-7 (pbk.)

    1. War brides – Canada-Biography. 2. War brides – Great Britain – Biography.
3. Women immigrants – Canada – Biography. 4. World War, 1939-1945 –
Personal narratives, British. I. Title.

D810.W7G73 2002   940.53'082   C2002-900119-6

We acknowledge the financial support of the Government of Canada through the Book
Publishing Industry Development Program for our publishing activities. We further
acknowledge the support of the Canada Council for the Arts and the Ontario Arts
Council for our publishing program.

Typeset in Janson by M&S, Toronto
Printed and bound in Canada

McClelland & Stewart Ltd.
The Canadian Publishers
481 University Avenue
Toronto, Ontario
M5G 2E9
www.mcclelland.com

2 3 4 5 6   07 06 05 04 03 02

Introduction

"Blimey! We were a rum bunch!" proclaimed a beaming Winnie Field of Manitoba after she watched her daughter portray her in *The Light in Winnie's Window*, a musical about the war bride's life. It was all there on stage in 2001: the young woman in uniform "for the cause" nearly sixty years before, her meeting with a handsome Canadian soldier at a dance, the marriage, the baby, the journey from Britain to Canada, and the surprises that greeted her upon her arrival.

The audience alternately dabbed at tears and roared with laughter at Winnie's plight onstage, and at the end of the evening there was a palpable sense of wonder that this woman, these women, had done something a younger generation could not imagine doing. Little realizing it at the time they left home, the war brides have become heroic figures.

Canadian servicemen stationed in Britain during the Second World War (1939–1945) spent a great deal of their time waiting, waiting for everything from showers to their European troop assignments. The ensuing boredom was relieved in part with visits to canteens and service clubs, where the local young women, among them shop girls and those who were working in various capacities for the government (such as the Land Army and the WAAF), also went for entertainment and diversion. These young women, some still in their teens, may have walked to the dance in a gaggle of giggling friends, but there was a chance they would leave the hall with a new friend, a Canadian with "a wonderful accent," or "bright blue eyes," who would later become their husband.

For some, there was time for the slow evolution of a romance with a serviceman who was billeted at a local estate. Numerous letters were exchanged and every opportunity to spend time together eagerly taken. There were walks and furtive embraces on roads pitch-black for national security reasons. There were also chaperoned visits with family members who had a talent for instantly knowing that the young soldier and his girl were a perfect match. But often, there wasn't time for a long engagement. Love grew quickly when bombs fell and lives could end at any moment. Servicemen were far from the comforts of home; a ready smile, some lovely gams, and a home-cooked meal restored the soul and quickened the heart. "They were different times," is an oft-heard refrain from the brides and their husbands. "You never knew how much time you had."

Marriages were often performed as quickly as they could be arranged, given family situations and military requirements. Women borrowed wedding dresses, or made fashionable coats out of dyed army blankets. A spray of flowers garnished their lapel and shiny silver cardboard horseshoes were given and carried for luck. Brief honeymoons were enjoyed before the inevitable separations occurred. Husbands left for battle not knowing their wives were pregnant. Babies were born and not seen by their fathers for years, and sometimes never. Wives became single parents trying to cope with new motherhood when they'd scarcely had time to enjoy married life. Who *was* that man, really? Who would he be when he returned?

When the war ended, there was time to bring these families together. Canadians had married women from Britain, the Netherlands, France, Germany, Belgium, Norway, Sweden, and Italy. Often with only a few hours' notice, these women packed what they could and slipped away without time for the goodbyes they might have wished for. No public celebrations for their new life were allowed for security's sake. The pain of the leave-takings is one of the most pervasive elements of the war brides' stories. Nearly sixty years later, they still weep as they recall parents waving goodbye, the final glimpse of siblings who didn't know it was the last time they would be together.

Like pioneering women before them, the British war brides, nearly 48,000 of them, sailed across the Atlantic armed only with a perfunctory knowledge of their new home – and often of their new husbands. Camouflaged ships that had transferred Canadian servicemen overseas from Halifax were returning with their wives and some 22,000 children – Canadians all. Pier 21, the waterfront shed that had been one of the last places glimpsed by their departing husbands, became the depot for the arriving families. And what a disappointment! Where were the cowboys? And the igloos? Had their husbands really been pulling their legs? And who was that fellow with the brown fedora? It was easy not to recognize a man you hadn't seen for two years, especially when he wasn't wearing brass-buttoned, government-issue clothing from the outside in, so to speak.

And the trains! Who knew a country could be this big!

The following stories are from war brides who survived their voyage of a lifetime to Canada. They are the women whose strength of spirit, love, and commitment to life often brought them through hardships not unlike those of Canada's earliest settlers. Nothing, not even the multitude of government pamphlets and documents these women read before their journey, could have prepared them for what lay ahead. Some, city-born, became sodbusters whose cardboard wedding horseshoes were traded in for real horseshoes on real horses. Many were not welcomed, by their new relations, or by communities who disliked their "foreign-ness." Some of their husbands died before they'd been in Canada for a year. Some were beaten, others abandoned. Some couldn't wait to get back to England; others never wanted to return. Canada had become home.

Despite the haste of some of the marriages, many of the war brides and their husbands have celebrated sixty years of wedded life. They take special pride in what they made of their lives in Canada. They have retained their traditions and at the same time absorbed the changing trends. (As one war bride recently wrote, "Nova Scotia War Brides Rock!") Their contribution to this country has been celebrated with reunions and, in 2000, by the mounting of a memorial plaque at Pier 21, where they first stepped ashore. They themselves would say, "Who knew? All we did was marry our amazing Canadians!"

Their stories, often woeful but inevitably spiked with humour, merit our attention and our tears, our appreciation and our laughter. Winnie Field put it well – they're a "rum bunch" all right!

As wife of the Governor-General of Canada I have been asked to write a short foreword to this booklet, which has been prepared by the Canadian Government for the help and guidance of British wives of Canadian servicemen about to make their homes in this country.

Having spent the last four years in Canada travelling East and West, North and South, I have a pretty good idea of what my fellow countrywomen will feel when they arrive and what the people are like with whom they have come to live. So I would commend this booklet, which is full of useful information, but is rather too modest in stressing the great kindness of the people and how ready they are to welcome every stranger who is willing to make friends and who wants to like Canada.

Of course, everyone will feel strange at first because it is a new-world country and the distances and size of it are so tremendous that no amount of preparedness can begin to make one realize that. For instance, several of the provinces are each larger than Britain and France put together; and so it is to be expected that each province has its own special characteristics and interests.

Take, for example, two alone. Quebec is almost entirely Roman Catholic and French-speaking. It is watered by thousands of lakes and rivers. Manitoba, on the other hand, is a prairie province. It is flat as can be, with endless miles of wheat land as far as the eye can see. It is predominantly Protestant.

I mention these two as they are such a contrast; but each province is different. So wherever one may make one's home one's loyalty is to Canada and one's province; but in whatever part of Canada you go to live you will find friendliness, a welcome, and the opportunity to make for yourself and your family a happy future.

So good luck to you all.

Alice Mary Countess of Athlone -

The official photograph of the Countess of Athlone counters the warmth of her best wishes for the war brides. From "Welcome to War Brides," 1944.

BERYL AFFLECK

I was part of a small group of husbands (mostly Canadian officers who had served with the British Armed Forces) and wives travelling together to Halifax aboard the *Queen Mary* in August 1946. We had little advance notice of our sailing and arrived in Portsmouth after a hectic trip from my home in Chester. We were on our way to Canada a few hours later. I didn't go back home again for fourteen years.

My husband, Hugh, who was in the Royal Navy, had the idea that if I kept moving in the fresh air I wouldn't get seasick. Though it seemed to me at the time that I walked most of the way across the Atlantic, I definitely did not get seasick.

On our morning hikes around the upper deck, we met two elderly gentlemen who were also taking their constitutional walk. They wore long dark overcoats and black homburg hats, which were politely lifted to us every time we passed. It was a couple of days before we learned that the gentlemen were Mr. Mackenzie King, the prime minister of Canada, and his finance minister, returning from a meeting with Winston Churchill in London.

Cunard R.M.S Queen Mary

We docked in Halifax late at night. By two o'clock in the afternoon, we were going ashore in the pouring rain. As Hugh and I headed down the gangway, we saw the huge nets hauling baggage out of the hold and we watched in horror as one load swung against the side of the dock. We recognized a large sea chest belonging to us. We had packed it with great care just a few days earlier. It split open, and silverware, china, books, and pictures, all our precious memories, dropped into the dark, oily waters of Halifax Harbour.

I couldn't believe what was happening to me. I hadn't even set foot on Canadian soil yet! All my mother's dire warnings about this "wild new country" rushed into my mind. But there was no time to reconsider – the train was already sounding its whistle and we had to get on board. Before I knew it, Hugh and I were on our way to Toronto and a whole new life, with only what we carried in our hands.

Looking back, I can see that we were no worse off than most of the early immigrants to Canada who arrived with what they could carry, but at the time it was devastating. I didn't sleep much. As day-light came, I looked out the train windows and saw endless stretches of dark trees and rushing rivers, but no towns or people.

When we came into Quebec, I was reassured by the little villages clustered around the tall, white churches. In Montreal, we tried

Prime minister William Lyon Mackenzie King, broadcasting a message to Canada on VE Day, 1945.

to phone Hugh's family, but there was no reply, so we got back on the train.

Around suppertime that day, we pulled into Toronto's Union Station, where I was overwhelmed by the high vaulted ceilings, the shiny floors, and the big, clean windows, so different from the darkened wartime stations back home. Again, we phoned Hugh's family; again, no reply. So we took a taxi out to the Beach part of the city. The family had moved during Hugh's six years overseas, so he was as lost as I was. We didn't realize until then that it was the Labour Day weekend and folks were returning from their summer at the cottage.

So what did we do? Well, we broke into the house through the milk box, opened the back door, and went in. I remember the hushed quiet of the house, the drawn curtains and the smell of wax. We were so tired that we ate some cheese and crackers and fell asleep on the big couch in the living room. Several hours later, we were awakened by Hugh's parents and a large collie dog, whose wet tongue on my face was a lovely welcome. They hadn't expected us to arrive so soon, and there we were – a son returning after so many years and an unknown daughter-in-law. What a night that was! We talked until the wee small hours and then settled into a comfortable bed for the first time in almost two weeks.

The meat shortages, and wartime humour, continued.

Eventually, life settled down and we began to make a home of our own up on the third floor of the family's house. Soon the winter came, and I was introduced to winter boots, toques, and "snuggies." How I laughed at the idea of pulling them on and off, but I soon appreciated their value when the temperature dropped. I loved the snow. The dog and I went for long walks every day. Folks thought it was strange that I would just "go for a walk," but at home we never had a car and walking was the only way to get around.

I soon began to think about Christmas. Letters every week from my mum and dad were my lifelines to home, and I was determined to make my first Christmas in Canada a special one for the family I had left behind. Everyone in Canada seemed to have so much, and though they spoke of rations and shortages, they had no idea what the words really meant. I packed box after box with food and treats, including lots of tea and sugar for my mum; cheese; and tobacco for my dad. I also packed toys and clothes for my young brother, who had only known wartime Christmases.

Christopher Vickery and his mother celebrate their first Christmas in Canada, 1945.

When Christmas Eve came, I went to church with a happy heart, knowing that back in Chester, it was going to be a truly merry Christmas. It was snowing again in Toronto on Christmas morning, and down in the living room there was a huge tree covered with lights and decorations. Underneath the tree there were piles of gifts, all wrapped in bright paper. Hugh's dad acted as Santa Claus and handed out parcels to everyone in turn. We had only given small gifts to each other back at home, so I was overwhelmed by all the packages. There was clothing, things for our flat, chocolates, and even gifts for the baby that was due in the spring. I went from tears to laughter and back again all day long.

Christmas dinner was a feast that included my first taste of cranberry sauce. At each person's place at the table there was a small red candle in a brass candlestick, and as the meal began, the candles were lit. We watched them burn throughout the meal. I was told that the person whose candle lasted the longest was assured of a long and happy life.

*Yes, a lot of things are different here but you will find a lot
of things that are very like they were at home. . . . You will find
little mention of them, for the purpose of this book is rather
to provide a guide to the things that are different and to give
you recipes for dishes that are likely to be among your
husband's favourite things to eat.*
— CANADIAN COOK BOOK FOR BRITISH BRIDES

JOYCE ANDERSON

I was born, an only child, in 1927 in a stone cottage near Whitby. My father was a mechanic and had served in the First World War. My mother died when I was only five years old, and I went to live with my grandmother. My father remarried and I returned to my family's home. When I was twelve, the war broke out. I remember the day war was declared. It was a beautiful Sunday.

My father was working as a chauffeur for a woman who lived not far from my grandmother's house. His employer invited me to stay at her house for a few weeks and visit with my father. In 1943 my father died of an aneurysm three months before my stepbrother's birth. My grandmother took charge of me again. She decided I had enough family misfortunes. I was sixteen.

I was in school for most of the war. There were no air-raid shelters nearby, so the beginning of the school year was delayed for a full semester while shelters were built. My grandmother lived among several major airfields, so we were not bombed and bothered by the Luftwaffe. I remember the first time I tried on a gas mask – I detested the thing!

The bread we ate looked like they had dropped the flour on the floor and then swept it up and baked it into a loaf. It was a dirty shade of grey. The gorgeous white buns they served on the *Aquitania* when I came to Canada were quite a contrast!

I met my husband, Ross McLennan, at a dance in 1944. He was from Bracken, Saskatchewan, and was a fitter for the Royal Canadian Air Force. We were able to have a few dates, but I wasn't thinking about getting married. I was having fun. On a starry night, he proposed to me during the walk home after a dance. It came as a surprise. I told him I had to think about it.

I accepted his proposal the next day! My grandmother objected at first. I think she probably didn't want to be left on her own. But we worked it out with some discussion and debate. Ross and I were engaged in 1945. He left for Canada about a month and a half after the war ended in Europe and returned to his farm in Saskatchewan. We had not yet married.

I had to go to Sackville House to get information, and I needed medical clearance. There were forms to fill out and a waiting list to get onto. My grandmother, despite her early opposition, paid my passage to Canada. After an eighteen-month wait, I received a letter that gave me ten days' notice for my departure. I travelled "wartime first-class." The sleeping quarters were crowded, but we had excellent linens and good food, which I enjoyed because I didn't get seasick.

From 1944, the Canadian Wives' Bureau was located in Sackville House, near Piccadilly Circus in London.

There was a spot just outside the dining room that seemed to be a "make or break" point for those who were seasick; they would either break down there or be able to make it through the meal.

I remember how the *Aquitania* entered Halifax Harbour as the sun was setting over the city. We were processed on board the ship and walked straight through the cavernous Pier 21 building and straight onto the train. As it was New Year's, we had a bit of a celebration. I was startled by the porters on the train: they were all black, which came as quite a surprise.

The train stopped in Winnipeg, where I managed to freeze my nose during a brief jaunt off the train. I had received a telegram that told me to get off at Moose Jaw, Saskatchewan, so when we arrived I got off and looked around. I was chatting with two policemen when my fiancé showed up, and joked that he didn't know whether to claim me or sneak off!

We were married on January 16, 1947. It was a very small wedding. My mother-in-law was not certain I would make a good farmer's wife. My reaction to the Prairies? You could see for miles and miles – but see what?

I had to learn to bake in Canada, and under rationing it was impossible to teach someone to cook, because everything would go to waste if you spoiled a recipe.

We had a very small house and we farmed until 1963. My grandmother died in 1959 and left me an inheritance. My husband wanted it in his account, and I refused. Our marriage ended, and I went to Saskatoon to learn to teach. I taught in Central Butte and Stanley Mission, and then I went to work at a variety of places in the North. My specialty was English, but I also taught grade school. In time, I got married again.

I didn't return to England until 1999. I had tracked down my half-brother on the Internet, and I went to meet him. We are twenty years apart in age and had never met, so I was surprised by how remarkably similar we are in manner and appearance.

*Some women,
like Mrs.
E. A. Stevens,
were reunited
with
injured
husbands,
1946.*

JOYCE BECK

I remember thinking how white the bread rolls were when we went for our first meal on the *Queen Mary* in 1946. It turned out to be my only meal on the voyage, as I was seasick for the first five days crossing over to Canada. The other war brides looked after my fifteen-month-old son, David, as I could not get out of my bunk.

When I arrived in Halifax, my husband, Lester, was very sick with tuberculosis that he caught in France during the war. I stayed with my mother- and father-in-law and their family for ten months. Then I moved to the Annapolis Valley, Nova Scotia, to be near my husband, who was in the hospital there for two and a half years. When he got out, he could not work for another two and a half years. But I am happy to say that we have now celebrated more than fifty years of marriage.

*Because of war conditions we have all had to get used to
"waiting." You wait to go aboard ship, you wait to get off,
you wait for the special train to pull out of the station, you wait
to get into the dining-car on the train, you even wait your
turn in the washrooms. This, however, will not be new to you
as doubtless you are accustomed to queueing up.*

— WELCOME TO WAR BRIDES

BETTY BEZANSON

In the early days of the war, women as well as men were called up. I was about seventeen when I went to work at No. 15 Canadian General Hospital in Bramshott. The Canadians wounded at Dieppe were sent there. The hospital was run by nursing sisters, and we would try to make conditions as comfortable as possible for the nurses. We all lived at the military base.

I met my husband, Arthur Bezanson, at a dance in 1941. I watched him, and when "ladies' choice" was called, I tapped him on the shoulder. From then on we had every dance. Arthur wanted to see me again and said he'd take the bus to the little town where I lived. One time we met and went walking through the local park. All of a sudden, I could see my parents ahead of us and thought I might be in trouble, but my mother looked up and we had to continue walking. I introduced Arthur to my parents, and my father was wonderful to him.

Arthur played the drums in a military band that provided music for a lot of the dances. His commanding officer would let him leave the drums for the last waltz so he could dance with me. I sat there all evening, waiting for just one dance.

It was very scary in the blackouts. One night, Arthur and I were walking to the theatre and he lit a cigarette. Out of nowhere, a hand came over his shoulder and a voice told Arthur to put out the cigarette. It was a policeman. It was so dark we hadn't seen him. The police would knock on doors if they could see a crack of light coming out of your house.

Arthur wrote a letter to my parents, saying how much he loved me and that he would take good care of me. He said that he would do everything he could to make sure I got back for a visit. Arthur wrote the letter before we were married, when he was nineteen. I didn't know the letter existed until my mother died and I returned to England. I found it in a Bible on my mother's bedside table.

Our wedding day was February 9, 1944. You couldn't get nylons in England, so Arthur's mother sent over two pairs to me as a wedding present. I wore a white dress and carried a prayer book with ribbons and white roses hanging from it. My two sisters were my bridesmaids.

We were getting off the train for our honeymoon in London when a "doodlebug" went past. Arthur pulled me to the ground, but when I got up the knees of my nylons were ripped. I was so angry with Arthur for ruining them!

We stayed in London only for one night and then moved on to Blackpool for two weeks. We shouldn't even have stayed in London for that one night, because bombs were dropping. The hotel kept telephoning our room, asking us to go to the shelter, but Arthur refused.

Arthur was stationed quite near me at first, and then he was at Aldershot, but could get home on weekends. I was able to see him frequently. Arthur was supposed to be going back to Canada in November. I was pregnant and wanted the baby to be born in England, where my mother could help. The officials told me that if they could, they would put me on a ship to Canada before I was six months pregnant, but I was further along by the time I got word to go, so I had to stay behind in England.

My husband went to his commanding officer in Aldershot and said he was not going back to Canada until after the baby was born.

ALDERSHOT, VICTORIA ROAD   85554

They let him stay in England. Our son Barry was born in November 1945, and christened in February of 1946.

We had an apartment, and I tried to save the good food for when Arthur came home for the weekend. One weekend, I had everything ready and I was waiting, but he didn't come. I spoke to my neighbour, who eventually told me that Arthur had left for Canada without telling me because he couldn't stand saying goodbye.

I sailed to Canada with Barry on the *Letitia* later that year. After I was notified that it was time to leave home, I went to London to stay at a hostel, supposedly for one night. We stayed there for four days, and I wanted to go home. I was on the ship with about two or three dozen other war brides, and I found the trip difficult because there were so many babies and children. There were no such things as disposable diapers then, so my mother cut out squares of cloth and told me simply to throw them overboard when they were dirty!

I worried that Barry might get sick on board. The doctor told me he wouldn't, but that I might. I did feel squeamish a few times, but was never sick. Barry was sick the whole time, though, so I took him to the ship's doctor. It turned out Barry had cut two teeth. I was told not to nurse him any more, that the seasickness was passing through my milk to Barry. For the seven days of the journey, I had to feed the baby weak tea with lots of sugar. He lost weight but was okay.

The morning before we landed in Halifax, we had to go and exchange our English money for Canadian money at the purser's office. After we docked at Pier 21, they announced the names of the women who were to come up on deck. I gave one woman a picture of Arthur and asked her to go upstairs and look for him. She came back but had been unable to find him. Then I went up, looked for him, and couldn't see him because there were so many people. The other woman's name was called and she left. Finally, my name was called, and they told me that my train was waiting. I knew something was wrong, because Arthur had said he would meet me.

I decided not to go up on deck. The purser came down and took me off the ship, but Arthur wasn't there. The women had been told that the duty of the day for the soldiers working at Pier 21 was to help war brides and their children. A soldier came up, took my bags, and told me to follow him. I opened my purse to give him a tip, but I didn't understand Canadian money, so I just held up a bill with a five on it. Then a hand reached over my shoulder and took the money. It was Arthur! He passed the soldier a smaller tip.

We lived with Arthur's parents for about a year, and then we built a house in Westville, Nova Scotia. I found the food in Canada very different. We war brides had been given pamphlets that told the women not to feed their husbands certain things. We had been living with Arthur's parents for a while when Arthur asked me to make a jam sponge. That was one thing I was good at making. So I made it, but it turned out flat – the flour in Canada wasn't "self-raising," it had no baking powder in it.

Language was different, too. In England, if a woman's husband has a good job, people say he "makes a good screw." One day, I was talking to my new neighbours in Westville, and I mentioned to a woman that her husband must make a good screw. The woman became distant, and I didn't know what was wrong. I told Arthur what I'd said, and he explained I shouldn't say that in Canada!

Our son, Brian, was born in October 1947 and our daughter, Janie, in November 1955. I meet once a month with a local group of war brides and attended the reunion in Halifax in 2000. Canada is a lovely country, and the people were very good to me when I arrived. After Arthur died, some people thought I would go back to England, but I love Canada.

The average Canadian dislikes boiled fresh meat almost as much as he dislikes suet pudding, though he usually likes boiled meats that have first been corned, cured or smoked.
— CANADIAN COOK BOOK FOR BRITISH BRIDES

JEAN BOCK

Friday, April 26, 1946
I left Sheffield at 9 a.m. and was met in London by the Canadian Army and driven in a private car along with a girl named Beatrice to the hotel. This place is very nice and quite near Hyde Park. We slept in two-tier bunks along with about two dozen other girls, including Margaret from Scotland. We three became great friends. We also made friends with six Dutch girls and on Friday afternoon we all went out together. On Friday night there was a Cinerama show in the lounge. On Saturday we were allowed to go out all day until 8:30.

We went with Beatrice to her sister's at Hammersmith. Then we went to see Bette Davis in *The Corn Is Green*. After that we had supper at a café and so back to the hotel.

Sunday, April 28
Sunday morning we left the hotel in private motor coaches for

Waterloo. We boarded the special train for Southampton and after getting our passports, etc., we went aboard the ship. This was a thrilling moment. I walked up the gangway and a steward took my bag and showed me to my cabin. I am on A Deck, next to the Purser's Cabin, in B Cabin. I share this with twelve more girls. The beds are wonderful and soft and everything is very clean. I am second sitting so I went down with my friends to dinner at 7 o'clock. I chose soup, chicken, roast potatoes and vegetables, ice cream, tea, and an apple. Then we walked the decks until bedtime.

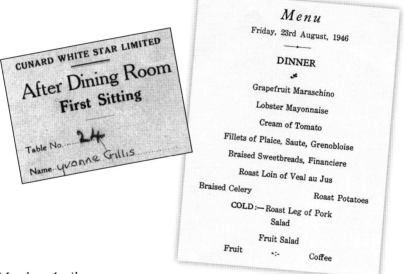

CUNARD WHITE STAR LIMITED

After Dining Room
First Sitting

Table No......24

Name......Yvonne Gillis

Menu

Friday, 23rd August, 1946

DINNER

Grapefruit Maraschino

Lobster Mayonnaise

Cream of Tomato

Fillets of Plaice, Saute, Grenobloise

Braised Sweetbreads, Financiere

Roast Loin of Veal au Jus

Braised Celery   Roast Potatoes

COLD:— Roast Leg of Pork

Salad

Fruit Salad

Fruit   ·:-   Coffee

Monday, April 29

Monday morning we were awakened by a voice at the microphone saying, "6:30, time to rise and shine, come on girls, get out of bed." We were up on deck by 7:30 and our breakfast was at 9 o'clock. I chose oranges, wheat flakes, two eggs, bacon and toast, and tea. The food is wonderful and we have a very nice waiter at our table.

We went on deck and had a lifeboat drill. We did look like freaks. At noon we sailed. It was a wonderful experience. As the boat sailed out, the girls sang, "There'll Always Be an England." People on the docks waved and cheered and we did the same.

The gift shop opened at 4 o'clock and we got Coca-Colas and chocolate, nail-varnish remover, lipstick, handkerchiefs, etc. We had lovely meals again, always with plenty of fresh fruit. At night we had community singing.

Tuesday, April 30

Most of the girls are sick and I don't feel so good myself, but I manage to keep eating although I only had grapefruit and toast for breakfast and for lunch and dinner, cold salads. The dining room is almost empty at every meal. I stay on deck all day in the fresh air. The weather is glorious.

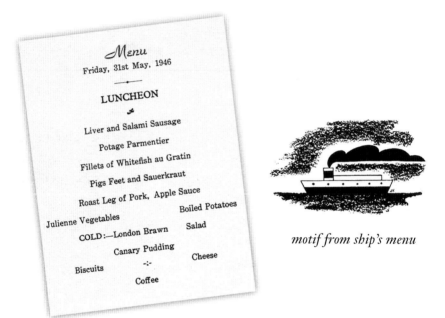

Menu
Friday, 31st May, 1946

LUNCHEON

Liver and Salami Sausage

Potage Parmentier

Fillets of Whitefish au Gratin

Pigs Feet and Sauerkraut

Roast Leg of Pork, Apple Sauce

Julienne Vegetables   Boiled Potatoes

COLD:—London Brawn   Salad

Canary Pudding

Biscuits   -:-   Cheese

Coffee

motif from ship's menu

Wednesday, May 1

A week today we should dock at Halifax. Most of the girls are very ill and my friends have been sick, but so far I'm eating lots of this good food. Oranges, peaches, apples, eggs – anything you wish. Everyone is very kind to us and the nurses are in attendance all the time. Wednesday evening we sat up on deck until 10 o'clock, wrapped in our dressing gowns, singing songs, and having lots of fun. The stewardess said once we get into the mid-Atlantic, it will be much calmer.

Thursday, May 2

We were awake by 6:30 and soon up on deck. By 7 o'clock it is much calmer and most girls have come down for breakfast. I ate oranges, Corn Flakes, two eggs, bacon, toast and marmalade, and tea. We came straight up on deck again and were interviewed by a pressman. Our names will be in the Canadian papers. We sit doing our embroidery. We have great fun. There are now eight of us, all good friends.

We put our clocks back 1/2 hour each day.

Friday, May 3

Up early once more. It was a lovely warm sunny day and we were out doing our embroidery all day on the deck and stuffing ourselves with fruit and chocolate.

Saturday, May 4

We ran into a storm and the boat heaved and plunged something terrible. The spray was coming right over the decks. Lots of girls were sick again, but I feel fine and I'm eating lots of good food, especially apples.

Sunday, May 5

It is much calmer now and the sun is coming out, but it's still very cold. I was up on deck by 7:30 a.m. I had a good breakfast – oranges, Corn Flakes, two eggs, bacon, toast, and tea.

This morning we went to the church service. It was lovely. We sang "For Those in Peril on the Sea," also "Through All the Changing Scenes of Life."

We sat on the deck all day. We had turkey, ice cream, etc., for dinner. Then we washed our hair – Bebe, Scottie, and me – and then went to bed. It was lovely.

Diana Lamont was born today. This is the first time a baby has been born on the ship so of course a great fuss is being made and a fund has been started in honour of her. Mrs. Lamont was in my cabin.

Tuesday, May 7

With a soldier for each girl, we left the ship and boarded the train and what trains – the comfort is wonderful. I am still with my friends. At the station, before the train left, we were given milk, wonderful milk, and cream biscuits.

The first stop was Moncton. We got out for magazines. It was snowing. We had bananas after dinner, then to bed. The beds are just wonderful.

Thursday, May 9

A lovely day. We stopped for 20 minutes at Quebec, a lovely city. At 7:00 a.m. Betty and I walked along the platform and were given oranges, nuts, gum, and chocolate, all free.

The next stop was Montreal. Beatrice and Betty left here for Toronto. We had four hours in Montreal and we were driven around town to see the sights and then to Eaton's – a big store where we thought we were in a dream. Everything you could imagine. I bought a blouse, undies, etc., rollers, and a nightdress, perfume, sweets . . .

Last night we passed through Ottawa, but I was asleep.

I posed for photos again. In the next place, we stopped for 20 minutes, almost all of the people were Indians. We were able to get bananas and ice cream and then on again for hours. We passed through forests growing close to the railway lines and beautiful lakes. To us, the scenery seemed wild and reminded us of the stories we had read of Indians, the tall dark pines, the calming shimmering lakes, and the wailing Whoo Whoo of the train as she roared on her way carrying us west, nearer and nearer to our journey's end.

In the fall of the year you will probably find yourself, like other Canadian wives, busy making pickles.

– CANADIAN COOK BOOK FOR BRITISH BRIDES

SOME TIPS ON PASTRY MAKING

★ Pastry dough made the day before is easier to handle and has better texture.

★ Have fat and water cold.

★ Be a miser with the flour used on pastry board and rolling pin.

★ Roll *lightly*, always from centre of dough towards edge, not back and forth; turn dough around but not over.

★ Don't stretch the dough to fit the pie plate.

★ Allow for the escape of steam; prick pastry shells; cut slits in top crusts before baking.

★ Always put pastry into a hot oven, 425°F. If pie has an uncooked filling cool oven to moderate heat, 350°F, after 10 or 15 minutes.

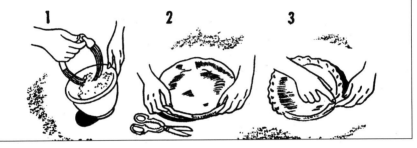

from "Canadian Cook Book for British Brides"

HILDA BRADSHAW

I was lucky, having been a boarder in a military school in the Nilgiri Hills in southwest India (my father had been in the British Army in India before she got her independence in 1947), but this would have been the first time a number of the "war brides," as we were named, had been parted from their families, which was hard for them.

From Halifax, I took the train to Saskatoon, Saskatchewan, and was tickled to see a city so clean after grimy London. I was disappointed to find out that we were not going to live in Saskatoon, but that I had another train journey to Carrot River, of all places. This was news to me.

We arrived in Carrot River in darkness, and my husband and I were met by my father-in-law and an older English couple who had a car. We drove out to the farm we were going to live on (another surprise!) along a dirt road, which was very narrow, and there was thick brush on either side. Imagine my thoughts, surrounded, except my for husband, by complete strangers, My father-in-law was a very sweet person, but he had said, "Let's get her home tonight before daybreak, because if she sees Carrot River in the daylight she'll go back right away." We laughed about that years later.

However, I did stay, and I learned to do everything a farm wife was supposed to do: canning, bread making, pies and cakes, making butter, and all the rest of it. I learned a lot, and people were so helpful. We were well received on the whole, but there were some girls who were not well received by some Canadian families, sad to say.

You are going to like Canada and Canadians. British brides who have preceded you, both in the last war and this, have made many fine friends and helped to pave the way for you.

— WELCOME TO WAR BRIDES

SHEELAGH BRUNELLE

My husband, Guy, was in the 1st Canadian Parachute Battalion attached to the British 6th Airborne Division. Soon after we were married in 1945, he returned to Canada. I had to wait until our baby daughter was five months old to make the voyage to Canada in August 1946. As much as I longed to be with him, I was extremely sad to be leaving my parents and family. In those days, to cross the Atlantic was like going to the other side of the world, with little hope of returning to England for many years. When my father died in 1948, I did come home for a long visit.

When we set sail that August, we were under the impression that it was refreshingly cool in Canada, and I thought that I would have to take a fur coat. Fortunately, I was not wearing it when we arrived in Halifax.

The voyage was rather difficult. There were ten girls in our cabin and two or three babies, and the water that we used to prepare their bottles was rusty. Nearly all of the other brides were Dutch, so there was a language difficulty, but the *Mauretania* was a beautiful ship, even when fitted as a troopship. The dining room was so impressive, and the food, after five years of rationing, seemed wonderful.

At last we sailed into Halifax Harbour. It was a lovely sunny day, and our first sight of Canada was the dark evergreens on the shore of the blue sea. It was exactly as I had imagined my new country. Point Pleasant Park is one of my favourite places in Halifax, my favourite Canadian city. Of course, I may be prejudiced, because it is the home of our youngest daughter, her husband, and our four grandsons.

I have to admit that even though I got a great welcome from my husband and his family, I was homesick for England for quite a few years. Of course, now Canada is indeed my "home and native land."

Sausages or bacon are often served with pancakes, but don't forget the [maple] syrup even then. The combination does sound odd but when you've tried it you'll agree that it's good.
— CANADIAN COOK BOOK FOR BRITISH BRIDES

ANNE CAVANAGH

It was a cold morning in March 1944 when the *Britannic* pulled out of the Liverpool docks. I had such a feeling of desolation as

LANDING STAGE, PIER HEAD, LIVERPOOL.

I waved goodbye to my family. How fortunate I was to have my husband, Bob, at my side. It was close to the end of the war, and his flying days were over.

The voyage was long, about ten or twelve days, as we had to zigzag all the way to Canada, to avoid U-boats, we were told. Three destroyers were on each side of the ship, so we felt safe. A day before getting into Halifax, our six ships sounded their tooters, turned around for home, and left a bunch of lonely war brides.

We had life drill twice a day. We stuffed ourselves with white bread and real butter – generally made pigs of ourselves! A few hours after having been deserted by our escorts, guess what? A U-boat alert.

We were all herded to our cabins and told not to move from our bunks. My husband was on the other side of the ship. After a couple of scary hours the "all-clear" was given. We often wondered in later years why we had been prisoners below deck when we had spent many hours practising Alert drill. We could have at least had a chance to jump overboard in life jackets.

We arrived in Halifax and then had a long journey to Regina. There we were met by a woman who never tried to make me feel welcome or ever forgave me for taking her son. My year in Regina was the unhappiest year of my life. Thank God I had a wonderful husband. Within one year, my husband and child and I returned to England, where we stayed for three years. We returned to Canada and lived in Ontario for many years before moving to Alberta.

War brides were apt to be looked upon as strange people. I found Canadians to be more curious than friendly. I don't think too many of us figured we had arrived in the land of milk and honey.

Canada *has* been good to me. However, it has been good to me because I have been good to Canada. Along with my husband, I worked very hard for every dollar I made. We still have great get-togethers with the war brides' clubs, have reunions, and help each other out.

We have made many happy visits to England. Since retirement, we have travelled around the world and enjoyed life, four great kids, and nine grandchildren. Despite my long-departed mother-in-law, I have a great relationship with my husband's family.

A few years ago, Bob and I decided to go on a nostalgic trip from Edmonton, where we live, to Halifax. We went to the dock area, where there were a few touristy shops, and asked people in three places how we could get to Pier 21. None of them had heard of the spot.

I remembered it quite vividly. We had had to cross a railway line to get to the station, so we looked for a railway line and followed it, and lo and behold, it led us right to Pier 21. It was so dirty and eerie then, it scared me. I closed my eyes and tried to visualize all the immigrants, servicemen, and war brides who had set foot on this wonderful Canadian earth with such high hopes. I hoped that for the most part they had survived and found the happiness I had. [The restored Pier 21 facilities opened on July 1, 1999.]

But don't you think it's about time we all dropped the war "bride" thing? After all, my husband and I have now celebrated our fifty-seventh year of bliss!

·

*Of every ten Canadians, nine live within 200 miles of the
United States border and five of these live within 100 miles of it.
The lived-in part of Canada has been a horizontal strip just
north of the Canadian-American frontier, but in recent years
there has been a tendency to widen this northward.*
— WELCOME TO WAR BRIDES

·

JULIA MCCALLUM CONNELLY

Ben, as I called him, was really John Bernard Connelly in the Queen's Own Rifles, out of Toronto. He had been wounded and was recovering in Glasgow when we met. We were married New Year's Eve, 1945. Ben returned to Canada that July, and I awaited my turn to be sent over. In August 1946, I received word that it was time to go. I had to buy a few things, pack, say goodbye to friends and relatives. We weren't given much time to get ready. One minute I wanted to go, the next minute I didn't.

My father was not much for words. He was not much in favour of my marriage, either. He did give me some advice for the trip, though: "Keep eating on the boat. That way you won't be seasick." I didn't always take his advice, but I kept this in mind.

I never thought the time would come when I would leave my mother. She knew how much I loved this Canadian boy, and how much he loved me. She knew that my stubborn nature and sense of adventure would take me away. We didn't realize how heart wrenching the pain would be as the train pulled out of Glasgow station. My last view of my mother was of her running alongside the train as we both wept. It was the last time I saw her.

The *Queen Mary* was my ship, and it was filled with war brides, most alone, but some with one or two children in tow. Some were

Returning troops joyously disembark at Pier 21, the same pier from which they left for war.

pregnant. Most were from Scotland and England, some from France and Holland. Some girls never got on the ship. They stopped at the gangway and cried, not knowing what to do. As the band played "Auld Lang Syne," there was more crying. Those on shore cried because they were staying, and all of us on board cried because we were leaving. We were scared and already homesick.

I was bunked with a young Dutch girl. Ben had served in Holland. We tried to communicate, but she couldn't speak English and I couldn't speak Dutch. For once, I listened to my father and kept eating, hoping to ward off the seasickness. I was successful until the last day of the trip. I cried when I saw the vast amount of food available, knowing that the children at home were still on food rations, and here I was, eating like a queen.

As the *Queen Mary* pulled into Halifax Harbour the smell of rotting fish was overwhelming. The girls getting off to stay in Halifax were crying, thinking of living in a place with such a smell. A band greeted us, and it must have been a special occasion, for I think it was Prime Minister Mackenzie King who gave a welcome speech upon our arrival. He commented on being a bachelor, and one lass yelled out, "You're a wee bit late, chum, we're all spoken for!" That made us all laugh and took some of the tension out of the air.

We exchanged names and addresses and promised to write to one another. Then we went our own ways, with the Red Cross staff pointing us in the right direction. I went by war-bride train to Toronto. We got off the train at the Exhibition grounds, and that's where Ben met me. He had done his training for overseas on the same place, and he showed me the spot where he'd slept at the "Horse Palace." After a couple of days in Toronto, we headed to his parents' place in Havelock, outside of Peterborough, Ontario. We stayed there about six weeks. Then we got the travel bug and put our plans into action, heading to Northern Ontario.

Looking back, we were both adventurous. We raised our five children, travelled, worked, and lived all across Canada. From Gaspé Bay to Thunder Bay, from Pine Falls, Manitoba, to Mississauga, Ontario, and points in between. Finally, we settled in Parksville, British Columbia. I'm proud of my Scottish roots, but Canada's my home. It didn't matter where we were. If I was with Ben, I felt safe and loved and sometimes homesick, but always excited about the path that lay before us. I've never had any regrets.

———————•———————

On the prairies and in Ontario and Quebec there is usually snow from November to April and the thermometer frequently drops below the zero mark, but the sun is bright. You won't feel the cold as much as you may imagine from these temperatures — it's a "dry" cold for the most part and wonderfully exhilarating.

— WELCOME TO WAR BRIDES

———————•———————

Canadians are very democratic and take a dim view of people who try to impress them. They are, generally speaking, energetic and fun-loving. They'll join you happily in a good-natured "grouse" but it might be just as well to remember that they don't like criticism based solely on the fact that some Canadian customs may be different from those of other countries.

— WELCOME TO WAR BRIDES

PAULINE DUBUE

When I finally got my telegram to go to London, my mother was upset, but she bravely came with me, along with my good friend, to help me with the children. We said our tearful goodbyes, and then I was on my own with a great number of other girls. I was only twenty at the time, and my children were thirteen months and five months old. We stayed overnight in London, and what a time we had, lining up to go to the loo and to wash diapers and baby bottles. We got through it, though, and the next day we were put on buses that took us to Southampton and our journey to Canada.

It was an awful time on the *Aquitania*. I was seasick all the time. I would go up on deck with my children and had to sit down on the deck, as there were no chairs available. There, I would bring up my guts, and I swore that I would never set foot on a ship again – and I never have.

We arrived in Halifax on March 24, 1946. There was a band playing at the quayside, and soldiers were lined up at tables to take our entry cards. Two soldiers came up the gangway to help me carry my two children. As I presented my card and tickets, the young soldier asked, "So, how do you like Canada?" To which I replied, "I don't know. I just got here!"

We were put on westbound trains. Someone showed me where the water machine was so I could make hot bottles of milk for my infants. As we travelled overnight, the machine mysteriously disappeared. I had to walk down the train to the kitchen and timidly ask if I could make up the children's bottles. Of course, I had to put up with some whistles from the cooks!

We were overwhelmed by the vastness of the country. I expected to see Indians riding on horseback beside the train. It seems so funny now, after all these years. When we arrived in Ottawa, the Red Cross staff came on the train and helped us get our things together and carried the children out. There were crowds on the platform and everyone was clapping. I felt overwhelmed both physically and emotionally. When we got to my husband Jack's home, the family threw a big party for us.

I immediately joined the ESWIC (England, Scotland, Wales, Ireland, Canada) Club in Ottawa. It was a place for war brides to meet and feel at home. I met friends there and we have remained friends ever since. Canada is a great country, and I'm proud to call it home. My husband and I had six children, eight grandchildren, and two great grandchildren. My husband, who is missed terribly, died in 1988. We had a wonderful life, even if we did have some hard times.

MAVIS FALARDEAU

I married my husband, André, on October 31, 1945. He served with the RCAF as a Military Policeman in the City of York. At the time, I was employed as a saleswoman at York Co-op stores. As André was nearly every day on foot patrol on the streets of York, we saw each other often and developed a close relationship. After only three months, we married. My elder sister said to me at the time, "I don't give you more

than two months." Well, we are still together, happily married, and have no plan to separate yet.

My husband was repatriated to Canada on the *Île de France* in March 1946. I was left alone, waiting for my notice of departure from the Canadian Wives Bureau. I was about three months pregnant at the time, and lived with my mother. After many contacts and repeated requests to the Wives Bureau in London, I was finally advised to be ready to depart on twenty-four hours' notice. I was very relieved, as it was just before the time limit expired for allowing a pregnant woman to sail.

I sailed from Liverpool on the *Letitia* on May 12, 1946, and arrived in Halifax on May 21.

In Halifax, I was directed to a special war-brides train headed for Western Canada. Marvellous work and assistance was provided by the Red Cross, who did the impossible to make our arrival pleasant.

I found the journey from Halifax to Quebec very long and tiresome, but it was worth it. My husband was waiting for me at the train station at Lévis, just across the St. Lawrence River from Quebec City. I was also welcomed by his family, who could not speak English, so I tried to understand the best I could. (I now understand and speak French. After more than fifty years, who would not?)

As my husband could not find any decent lodging, we were invited to stay at his grandfather's twenty-four-room home situated in a residential section of Quebec City. (His grandfather owned the largest shoe factory in Canada at the time.) No need to say, we were well taken care of. We lived there for a year without rent, so it was a good start for us. The only trouble for me at the time was the language. I could not understand what everyone said, but I managed. I really felt welcomed.

After a year or so of trying, we managed to find our own four-room flat on the third floor of an old building in the centre of Quebec City. We acquired our own house four years later. We had a small family of four, two girls and two boys.

I visited my family only once in all that time. I am so afraid of flying. I don't think I'll ever see York again. This was my destiny.

Of course you will be lonely for your old friends and
for your family, and homesick for your country at first. . . .
Keep busy and interested, that's the best cure-all.
— WELCOME TO WAR BRIDES

MARGUERITE FEIST

I met my husband-to-be, Ted Feist, at a dance in southern England, where I was stationed in the WAAF in 1942. Our romance was brief, as his Canadian squadron was posted to Scotland after only three weeks of our knowing each other. He was later sent to North Africa and Europe, and over all that time we corresponded regularly. When

A Veteran at 20!

Back from scores of bombing raids over a dozen countries, this young airman has found adventure in the skies! Just out of his 'teens, an eager youth in years, he's a veteran in experience. He's a first-line fighting man, trained in the science of war at 5-miles-a-minute!

He and his buddies in R.C.A.F. air crew are team-mates. Gunner, Wireless Operator, Bomber, Pilot, Navigator— all work together as a smooth, swift "attack team" in a

giant bomber. Their targets surveyed in advance by daring reconnaissance pilots—their flight protected by the blazing guns of fighter planes—the bombers wing their relentless way to smash Nazi nerve-centres.

The expanded Air Training Plan has room for more men who want to be with these fighting comrades of the skies. Applications are being accepted for air crew duty, at R.C.A.F. Recruiting Centres throughout Canada.

If you are physically fit, mentally alert, over 17½ and not yet 33, you are eligible. If you are over 33, but have exceptional qualifications, you may still be considered. Lack of formal education is no longer a bar to enlistment.

WOMEN TOO— join "that men may fly." Canadian women fill vital jobs in the R.C.A.F. Women's Division, releasing men for air crew duties. Recruits are needed, age 18 to 40, physically fit, with at least High School entrance. Many useful and fascinating jobs await you. No experience needed. The Air Force will train you quickly to take your place with Canada's airwomen. Full information at any R.C.A.F. Recruiting Centre, or write address below for explanatory booklet.

ROYAL CANADIAN AIR FORCE
AIR CREW

AIR GUNNER · BOMBER · NAVIGATOR · PILOT · WIRELESS

FIGHTING COMRADES OF THE SKIES

For illustrated booklet giving full information, write:
Director of Manning, R.C.A.F., Jackson Building, Ottawa, or the nearest of these R.C.A.F. Recruiting Centres:
Vancouver, Calgary, Edmonton, Saskatoon, Regina, Winnipeg, North Bay, Windsor. London, Hamilton, Toronto, Ottawa, Montreal, Quebec, Moncton, Halifax.

he returned to England in late 1944, we met again and were married one week later. We had three months together in England before we sailed to Canada.

We travelled from Liverpool on the troopship *Louis Pasteur* on March 1, 1945. We arrived at Pier 21 on a grey, windy day on March 6. We were then escorted to the train bound for Edmonton, Alberta. The trip took five days and nights. I thought the journey would never end.

In Edmonton we changed trains for Grand Prairie, Alberta, and on to Wembley, a small village and my husband's home. I felt very fortunate that we had been able to travel together on this long journey. It was now March 12. I was welcomed by Ted's family, and six weeks later we started our life together on a 320-acre farm.

I soon learned how to become a farmer's wife, making bread, churning butter, and canning fruits and vegetables. There was beef, pork, and chicken to butcher, process, and put in sealers. It was hard work, as we had neither electricity nor running water, only a well. We did mixed farming for seven years, and finally gave up, as we never had a good crop. We were either hailed or frozen out. We lost quite a few cattle for a variety of reasons. I might add that our farm was three miles from the village and a mile from the nearest neighbours. It was a rather isolated life, but we were happy.

We had two sons, Tony and Dean, while on the farm. When it came time for schooling, we moved into Wembley, and my husband took over as the postmaster for three years. We had our third son, Stephen, in Wembley.

Such large quantities of fish are being sent to Britain and exported for Allied relief that there is not a great deal left for Canadians who live at a distance from the coast.
— CANADIAN COOK BOOK FOR BRITISH BRIDES

ODE TO A CANADIAN

He'll ruin your life, run off with your wife
And think he is doing no wrong.
He'll take you around if you lend him a pound
And take all you have for a song.

He's a thousand-mile ranch that was left by a chance
At the death of his old uncle Josh.
He's a marvellous shot, and believe it or not
Is a wonder at breaking a hoss.

He's forgotten his wife, he'll be single for life,
With the boys he's a regular guy.
And he's got a life story that is covered with glory,
But he's much too wicked to die.

He'll gaze with a frown on old London town,
Saying "Gee, what a helluva dump,
Why back home on my farm it would go in my barn"
And your ego goes down with a bump.

He has personal charm that is meant to disarm
To anyone that gets in his way,
And, don't listen to him, for he's only a whim
And he'll surely lead you astray.

Though you know he's a liar, your blood is on fire
As he whispers "I love you so much."
You go weak at the knees as he whispers "Oh, please"
And you feel his experienced touch.

Though you may regret it, you'll never forget it,
Although it is breaking your heart
To think of the kisses that other young misses
May give him while you are apart.

Though he makes you so mad, and often quite sad,
Still you cannot send him away.
He's really quite bad and a regular cad,
So why do you whisper "Please stay"?

He'll wed you, of course, when he gets his divorce,
So just think of this, when he begs for a kiss,
That a pram costs a helluva lot!

[author unknown]

IVY FELTMATE

MY HOME IN WORTHING, ENGLAND, 1943

Mother  *Father*

Brother Bob *Sister Ruby* *Brother Les*

ENTER MY CANADIAN ...

"Six Foot Two (plus) & Eyes of Blue" WOW
There goes Cupid!

Met his friends (Lloyd Bishop
died in the D-Day invasion)

April 22, 1944,
6 ½ weeks before D-Day

OUR DAUGHTER IS BORN AUGUST '45

Proud Father

A surprise Valentine photo for Daddy in Canada. Feb. '46

MY NEW HOME IN NOVA SCOTIA

"Banked" with sawdust, ready for winter. The woodpile our only fuel. No power. No running water. Outside "loo".

Uncle Ted holding Hazel

PERMISSION TO MARRY

During the period of your service in the Army, you may wish to get married. Before doing so, or before making any definite arrangements, you should be paraded before your Commanding Officer and request permission to marry. Your Commanding Officer will then make an investigation, and decide whether or not such permission may be granted.

This investigation is not carried out with any intention of "prying" into your private affairs, but is to protect you and your intended wife, and also to protect the Government. The Commanding Officer will assure himself that your intended wife is a suitable person, and one who can properly receive Dependent's Allowances. If she is under 21 years of age, he will require a certificate from her parents or guardian stating that they approve. He will require a certificate from some one like the lady's clergyman or doctor stating that she has a good character, and he will want to know what your financial standing is, and whether or not you have any debts. When he is satisfied, he will grant permission for you to marry.

It is most important that you receive the permission of the Commanding Officer before you get married. It provides a basis for documentation and allowances.

In addition to getting permission to marry from your Commanding Officer, you must of course, fulfil all the civil law requirements of the Province concerned, and procure a marriage license in the usual way.

NATIONAL WAR SERVICES

The Department of National War Services (Women's Voluntary Services) is making it possible for your dependents to have equal opportunity with their neighbours for leisure time activities and interesting recreational facilities.

Through unit auxiliaries, women's service clubs, fraternal organizations, welfare organizations, and other civilian and auxiliary services, parties, knitting groups, study classes, and recreational activities for children and adults have been organized for your dependents.

Don't worry, your dependents want you back, and while you're winning this war for them, they are being given every care and consideration by thoughtful "good neighbours."

KEEP YOUR MOUTH SHUT

Don't discuss, in public, movements of troops or ships. The importance of this cannot be over-emphasized. Don't talk "big" to impress people, especially girls.

Trains, busses, streetcars, theatres and beverage rooms are some of the places where your seemingly innocent conversation may be picked up by enemy agents. . . . Don't expect your wife, mother or sweetheart to keep a secret which *you* can't keep yourself.

Remember that old rhyme:

A wise old owl sat in an oak
The more he heard the less he spoke
The less he spoke the more he heard
Why can't we be like that old bird?

IRENE GRIFFIN

It was 1942 and a lovely Sunday afternoon when I met my handsome soldier. My plans that day were to go with my cousin Muriel to watch the Highland Regiments at Braemar, eighteen miles from Aberdeen, Scotland, where I lived. We would enjoy listening to the wonderful bands.

We usually rode our bicycles and made a day of it. This time, however, we decided to take the Blue Bird bus. While waiting for the bus, Muriel changed her mind about going. I was determined to go, so I jumped on the bus and it started away.

I stood hanging out of the bus door yelling for Muriel to come on until the bus reached the top of the street. I was furious with her and jumped off. As we were standing there, looking down into the beautiful Union Terrace Gardens, these two Canadian soldiers spotted us and said, "Come on down!"

There was a steep bank, so we said, "No, you come on up!" They did just that.

We were both stunned by these handsome soldiers with this wonderful Canadian accent. It started to rain, so we went down into the park shelter and spent a nice afternoon with them. We made a date to go dancing at the famous Music Hall. The boys' leave was soon up, and they went back to their camp in England. Gerald and I wrote letters and kept in touch until he had another leave.

After several months, Gerald and I decided to get married. In wartime, we were living for the moment, as we faced air raids and bombings on a regular basis. We also knew that servicemen would soon be facing heavy fighting in the front lines, so we wanted to enjoy what time we had together, in case it was short. I joined the NAAFI (the Navy, Army, Air Force Institute). We were attached to the forces. You were sent to wherever they needed you. I was sent to an air force base in Montrose, Scotland.

Our dress uniform was khaki in all the services. The most famous saying in the NAAFI was "a cup of hot water browned off and a rock," which meant "a cup of tea and a raisin biscuit." I worked mostly in the food ration stores.

In September 1943, my husband went to the front lines, after which, in March 1945, his unit went to the western front – Belgium, Holland, and Germany. He was with the 88th Light Anti-Aircraft Regiment. Since I was in Britain, we were able to spend seven days together, after which he returned to the front lines. Two weeks later, I boarded the troopship *Franconia*.

The ship was full of returning servicemen, war brides, and children. I left on March 28, 1945 and landed in Halifax on April 11. We were accompanied by a convoy, in case we were torpedoed.

Safe at last alongside Pier 21.

Canada's "National" game is hockey, a fast and exciting winter sport played on skates and somewhat resembling British field-hockey, which Canadians rarely play. During the winter there are frequent hockey league games in every city, town and village in Canada.

— WELCOME TO WAR BRIDES

LILIAN HALL

My father was head gardener for a big estate in Surrey, on the south coast of England. During the war, many estate owners moved elsewhere in England for safety, and their homes were used for billeting soldiers. In 1941, Victor Hall was with the Canadian West Nova Scotia Regiment, and he spent about eight months at the estate. We met just two weeks before he left for Europe. We kept in touch and were engaged in 1943, before Victor left for Sicily. We were married in 1945.

I was in uniform, because I worked for the Women's Land Army for about five years. Some girls married in uniform. Some rented wedding gowns and dry cleaned and returned them. But my friends gave me their clothing coupons so I could buy some white fabric and have my wedding gown made. I still have my dress.

Friends also gave me some of their food coupons, for butter and sugar, and my mum baked us a wedding cake. Everyone helped everybody else in those days. As Victor and I left the church after the ceremony, friends gave me silver paper horseshoes for good luck. I got at least four of them, and I still have them. Brides seldom if ever threw away their flowers. I still have some red rose petals from my wedding bouquet.

I recall arriving in London at our assembly point on April 25, 1946, only to be told that the crew of the *Letitia* had gone on strike for a day. So home I went, back to my family for the next twenty-four hours, only to face parting from them a second time!

We had on board two matrons caring for our needs. At the time, the show *Arsenic and Old Lace* was running in London, so we nick-named these two very efficient ladies for the women in the show. One was on night duty, the other on day duty.

Our fifth day on board was Easter Sunday. That day, my tummy received delicious cream cakes, the first in years. When I was sick that night, the matron insisted it was "seasickness," but I insisted it was "too many cream cakes."

My husband, Victor, met me right at Pier 21. I said farewell to four new-made friends who were travelling farther across Canada, and we promised to keep in touch every Christmas, which we have, since 1946.

I arrived at our home in Lunenburg, Nova Scotia, in 1946 – and it's been my home ever since. My late husband and I enjoyed many wonderful trips back to England.

You can take the gal out of England, but you can't take England out of the gal!

You must be prepared for greater informality in Canada than you have been used to and you will probably be asked countless personal questions. Your questioners are not being rude . . . they ask them merely because they are really interested in knowing all about you. Ask questions back, and you will see how gladly they respond!

— WELCOME TO WAR BRIDES

*Canadians with monthly incomes between $100 and $135 find
they spend from 30 to 40 per cent of their total income for food.
People living in cities and towns on smaller incomes may have
to spend as much as 50 per cent for food.*

— WELCOME TO WAR BRIDES

PAULINE HUNTER

My husband, Gerald Hunter, and I met on the Southampton ferry during the war. He was a sergeant in the North Nova Scotia Highlanders, and I was a Wren dispatch rider. He kindly helped me start my motorbike, which had stalled due to a long trip in the rain. A few days later, we met again on bikes, this time at the gas port, where the "boys" had waterproofed vehicles in preparation for the D-Day invasion.

It was May 1945 when we became engaged, and July 2 was our wedding day. The wedding was supposed to be June 26, but everything, flowers, guests, and reception, had to be postponed because Gerald's superior had to go on compassionate leave while they were in France. There were tears and a few frantic cancellations to be made – but all's well that ends well.

On June 23, 1946, I set sail from Southampton on the *Aquitania*. When I arrived at Pier 21 on July 1, it was a hot day, ninety degrees. Instead of seeing the expected cowboys and Indians in Halifax, I saw lots of people in shorts and sundresses. My husband and three of his relatives met me, and we drove up to Amherst. The car stopped, and my husband said, "We are home." I looked around and said, "But I thought you lived in a town?"

"We are in a town," was the reply. At that time, the roads were not paved and the house was next to a big pond.

The first year in Canada was the hardest. I had to adjust to my husband's family, and I was terribly homesick. After our first baby was born in 1947, times became easier and adjustments had been made. But it would be thirteen years before I saw my mother again. Life in Canada has been good for us, and I consider it home now. After fifty years, I would not want to live anywhere else.

MARGARET CHASE HUXFORD

On September 3, 1939, I was in Times Square, New York. I saw the declaration of war spelled out on the moving letters on the building. I should have been overwhelmed with dread at the news and perhaps have taken the next train home to Halifax, Nova Scotia. But this was the trip of a lifetime, my first bit of independence, and the chance to study art in summer school in this huge cosmopolitan city. I felt the British could get on without me for another three weeks, and so I stayed in New York City.

I remember with warmth the fact that everybody I had met and had become temporary friends with in the college and hostel was feeling so anxious for me, as if I were the only one in the entire United States whose native country was at war. I felt a little guilty that I was not feeling more anxious myself.

When I returned home to Halifax, I found the city coming to terms with its special role in the new war. With the enormous Bedford Basin, Halifax became a starting point for the all-important convoys that supplied Britain with food, materials, and personnel throughout the war. It became a regular occupation for the local people to climb Citadel Hill to watch the convoys and their eventual departure. As I watched, I had no idea that before the war was over I would watch my future husband set sail and then follow him myself a year later with our baby daughter.

In the meantime, my family, like many in Halifax, wondered how best we could contribute to the war effort. With two daughters in their mid-twenties, a small house, and a piano, we decided we would offer hospitality to the sailors as they waited for their ships to be refuelled and reloaded for the return journey. A local committee had been set up to co-ordinate this, and each Friday, my mother phoned to see who they had who needed some home comforts for the weekend. We could offer a hot meal, friendly conversation, a chance to show off at the piano, and the opportunity to flirt with my sister and me as we washed the dishes. Above all, we offered a glimpse of normal family life after so many weeks of danger and discomfort on board ship.

With no pubs and only one cinema that I can recall, Halifax was never the most lively of towns. With troops waiting to embark and sailors waiting for their turn-around, the city population grew four-fold. Most of our guests were English sailors, up to six at a time, and it took us a while to get it right. At first, my mother provided large helpings of wholesome home cooking. Then we realized that after the meagre rations they were used to, on board and back in England, they simply could not face so much. Indeed, the amounts were almost offensive.

The other main attractions at our house were the bath and the piano. I can still recall the heady scent of heavy wool uniforms, lived in and perhaps slept in for nine days at sea in crowded quarters. The odour filled the living room as we sat in easy chairs swapping stories. Also, the number of Englishmen who *thought* they could play the piano was legion. It must have been part of their naval tradition of military training, and they made enthusiastic use of my brother's upright piano. The music was pretty horrendous, but they enjoyed themselves, and it was our contribution to the war effort.

Another "attraction" was washing up after the meal. It's wonderful, what flirting can go on around the kitchen sink. They would offer to dry as my sister and I washed, and the arms would accidentally come round our waists as they reached to turn off the farthest taps.

Artist Robert W. Chambers paid tribute to the long hours of volunteer service given by the women of Halifax during the war.

Sometimes we liked it, sometimes not, depending on who was doing it, but we learned to deal with it all graciously.

Over the years, we entertained all ranks, shapes, and sizes. They suffered varying degrees of homesickness. Sometimes we would see our visitors only once, because they were sent on other duties or lost at sea. This was sad, but in those days it was a normal part of life and not too much was said. One group we saw more regularly were crewmembers of the HMS *Revenge*, which was a frequent visitor to Halifax. When they no longer came it was particularly noticeable.

Another regular visitor was a petty officer who I recall as looking rather like English actor and singer Harry Secombe. He had left behind in England a young pregnant wife, and he liked to sit quietly in an easy chair in the corner and knit little jackets and "soakers." On each of his visits, we heard the latest exploits of the new baby.

From time to time, we also put up any relatives who were passing through, as well as friends or acquaintances who had been given our address.

This weekend hospitality was strictly war work. Halifax in those days had a clear social structure, and even these restrained activities were frowned upon by some. During the week we pursued our own social life, and this tended to be with the officer classes. Officers and other ranks rarely moved in the same social circles, and although my mother was among the more liberal-minded of the time, to ignore this division would have caused extreme awkwardness.

During the war, I was a director of the College of Art in Halifax. My career advancement was in part because of the enlistment of some of my colleagues. Because I was an artist, and had visited New York City, I must have been considered rather bohemian by some, certainly by my rather better-behaved elder sister.

Many of the grander families, and organizations like the Masons, ran committees that organized dances and parties. The influx of eligible young men in their elegant uniforms was a heaven-sent opportunity for us, as partners were in short supply. Entrance was easier for engaged couples, and, as no one wanted to be seen to be encouraging loose living, I became "engaged" almost on a weekly basis. Drinking was forbidden, so we smuggled in our own bottles and kept them under the table. I am sure we fooled no one, but appearances were maintained.

I don't even remember the names of my numerous "fiancés," and our relationships were strictly proper, but when I did eventually, genuinely, get engaged, it was through the college rather than these social events.

The college was next to the City Parade and beside the Moirs Chocolates factory. As part of our war effort, the college offered evening classes for soldiers and sailors with time on their hands. I remember the college governors insisted on full blackout, and I had to arrange for huge rolls of black cloth for the high studio window. Among our students was a captain in the British Royal Regiment of Artillery who had great talent in sketching but tended to sketch me rather than the model or still life that was the subject for the evening.

Pat Huxford was in Nova Scotia to set up coastal defences, and in fact was going to set up an anti-aircraft battery on the lawn of my grandmother's house in Port Williams. So Pat was there long enough to ask me out and eventually asked me to marry him.

We were married in Halifax in June 1942. Ostentatious weddings were, of course, out of the question, but I had set my heart on lilacs for St. Andrew's Church on Coburg Road. Pat's colleagues borrowed a Jeep and drove around Halifax begging a branch wherever they saw a lilac bush in bloom. The church was full of lilacs, and I carried them in my bouquet.

General Elkins, who was Pat's commanding officer in the barracks at Sackville Street, and his wife were asked to act as Pat's parents at the wedding, as he had no family in Canada. I remember Pat telling me how he spent the previous Christmas walking the streets alone, watching families enjoying their Christmas meals behind half-drawn curtains.

After the ceremony, we rode in a Jeep to the bus depot where, still in our wedding outfits, we caught the bus to Annapolis Royal for our honeymoon.

Once back in Halifax, we moved into my parents' home on Vernon Street, in a more or less self-contained apartment of two upstairs rooms.

By Easter 1943, the threat to Nova Scotia was considered over, and Pat was recalled to work on the development of radar in Britain. My grandmother never did get her anti-aircraft gun.

While waiting to embark, the troops, including Pat, were collected in a transit camp outside of Windsor, Nova Scotia. A discreet tip-off gave me his whereabouts, and I got a ride out to find him on a hot summer's day. The sight of dozens of soldiers in their underwear, lying in their dormitory bunks as I walked in, is one I will not forget.

Some days later, I watched from Citadel Hill as his convoy sailed silently out of the harbour. By then, I was pregnant, and in November 1943 our daughter Ann Louise arrived at the Grace Maternity Hospital. It was still considered too dangerous for families to go to

England, but by September 1944, a growing stream of evacuated British wives and children was heading back across the Atlantic, and I decided to join them. The ideal moment seemed to be when Ann was still in a carrycot, but starting on adult foods. The very real risk of being torpedoed did not deter me, and no one tried to dissuade me from my intended journey.

Only my mother, father, and I knew the actual date of our departure. There was a slip of the tongue to my best friend who was sworn to secrecy. Everyone else, including Pat in England, knew only that I was due to cross towards the end of the year. I kept up the pretense by accepting invitations to farewell parties set for long after I was actually due to leave.

On the night of my departure (and in my first trouser suit), I took a taxi with Ann, my brother Bedford, and Pat's friend Charles Wise, who was also in the Royal Artillery. With this military escort, we drove through all the checkpoints without difficulty and up to the gangway. With everything in darkness, I had no idea where I was or what sort of boat I was on, but we were shown to a very comfortable first-class cabin for four, with a private bath. Only a lifebelt hanging on the cabin wall gave any hint that we were on the *Bayano*, a Fyffes Line banana boat, capable of carrying one hundred passengers.

We had previously invented a code so my sister, who worked for the Head of Signals in Ottawa, and my friend Faith's husband, who was in the Navy in New York, could trace my progress. Charles and Bedford then sent a telegram reading "BETTER ACT YOUR AGE NOT OLIVER'S." The first letter of each word spelled out the name of the boat. Unfortunately, Faith's husband forgot the code and telegraphed back "WHO THE HELL IS OLIVER!" while my sister, as ever, assumed I had made a mistake and tracked a different ship altogether.

I shared the *Bayano* with a hundred English mothers and children heading home, some of whom had already travelled 3,000 miles from the West Coast of Canada. We slept fully dressed, just in case, and met on deck every morning. We could see the convoy spread out around us. There were battleships and aircraft carriers and numerous corvettes, but still the U-boats got through, and every day we seemed to have lost more of the convoy. I recall signs on deck stressing "We *will not stop* if anyone falls overboard."

These mothers were wonderful to me, knowing better than me what it was like to leave family behind and go to a new country. They gave me advice and stuffed my pockets with half-crowns and pound notes so I could tip my way wherever I needed to go. Perhaps misled by the size of my cabin, they suggested I stay at the Adelphi Hotel when we arrived in Liverpool. One particular angel was Cecily Lee, who, despite having two children on her own and a husband to find, took me all the way to the Adelphi. We queued for rooms and I got the last one, just in front of the Belgian ambassador, who presumably had to find somewhere else. The room was fit for an ambassador, too, with separate lobby and bathroom all fitted out in old-fashioned splendour. Equally splendid was the housekeeper on our floor, who helped out with Ann until Pat arrived.

Ann had been in her "bunny bag" for several hours and was a bit of a mess, so I dumped her fully dressed into this elegant bath to get her clean. Bathtime over, Cecily got through to Pat's base in North Wales and passed me the phone. A lovely English voice said "Hello?" I assumed anyone with an English accent was Pat, so I said, "Darling, I'm here." The voice said, "I'm not darling, I'm afraid, but we have been expecting you. Pat's out for a walk, but as soon as we can get a hold of him, we'll let you know."

Women everywhere like to be dressed in the prevailing fashion and you will find that Canadian styles vary somewhat from those in Britain; moreover, clothing is not rationed in Canada, so if you wait until you get there you will avoid the difficulty of trying to eke out your coupons.

— WELCOME TO WAR BRIDES

EILEEN IRONSIDE

Our story is a fairy tale. My husband, Will, was born in Woolwich, London, and his family moved to Alberta in 1919. Will's father and my uncle had been school friends in England. After the war began, Will's mother kept saying to him, "When you go back to England, you must go see the Burchell family."

Will was a sergeant in the Army, in the Royal Canadian Medical Corps. In 1943, on his first leave in England, he came to our house. My mother was an invalid, so I'd decided to give up my career as a dress designer to look after her. I decided my mum was more important.

It was a pouring wet Saturday morning, around 8 o'clock. The bell rang. We lived in a quite big house with a gate in a high stone wall. The pull at the gate was broken, so I had to run out in the rain to open the gate. There stood this Canadian, and he just looked at me. I was looking at the most beautiful blue eyes I'd ever seen!

He told me who he was, and I told Will he'd better come in out of the rain. I ushered him into the sitting room, and I got my mother comfortable in a wheelchair. Then I left Mum and Will in the room to chat. I went to the kitchen; I thought I'd better make the poor soul something to drink. I made him a hot cup of Ovaltine, and gave him some of our wartime baking, which wasn't up to much.

Soon it was lunchtime and the gate bell rang again. It was someone sent by my brother, who was in the army in the Orkney Isles. He had managed to get a whole lamb from a farmer – half was for us and there was a note asking me to take the other half to his wife's family. My mum said to me, "You can take it, but you'd better take Will. It'll be dark when you come back, so take him to escort you." So I did. And after we had left my sister-in-law's parents that night, they said, "Bet you anything you like, those two are going to get married."

Will was only with us one day, but we wrote to each other, and he came back for his next leave. One of his brothers, and later another brother, came to visit. Every little while we had to look after them.

It just progressed from there. On January 13, 1944, Will and I were married at St. Mark's Church in Edinburgh. I designed and made my dress, because I couldn't buy one. I carried silver paper horseshoes for good luck, and gave them to someone after the wedding. Each year for twenty-five years, on our anniversary, we dressed in our wedding clothes. I wore my gown and Will wore his uniform. I made a special supper at home with whatever we had, made the table nicely. We stopped dressing up after the kids left home for university. Ten days after our fiftieth anniversary, a car ran into ours, and Will was severely injured and didn't survive.

After the war, Will came first to Canada. I said I wouldn't go until he was there to meet me. Before I could come to Canada, I had to go through terrible examinations. We had to go to our own doctor and to a Canadian army doctor, and then to hospital to make sure we were perfectly free of contamination or any diseases. Oh, golly, sitting there with all those women, to make sure no one had gonorrhea or any of that sort of thing. We also needed three character references from people who would say we were suitable to become Canadians. I wish I'd kept my one reference from the Bishop of Edinburgh. His words were "You'll be Canada's gain but Britain's loss." He married Will and I.

I made the trip from Edinburgh to Liverpool all alone and I cried all the way. From the moment I heard I was to leave until the day they had to carry me out of the house, I kept saying, "I'm not going." My dad said, "But dear, you're going to be happy."

I spent most of my voyage on the *Letitia* in the hospital, seasick. I thought it was going to be a nice cruise, but the first morning, I felt awful. My head was swimming. I asked for Corn Flakes and then ran out the door. I never did see Corn Flakes.

It was a twelve-day trip altogether – it took five days to cross Canada to Calgary. Will met me, then we went to Red Deer, where I met his parents and they took me to their farm in Blackfalds. I've been there ever since. I went from a home with everything to a farm with nothing. I didn't know a cow from a bull. I learned quickly. The farm was the biggest surprise – it was miles from everywhere and we were two miles from our nearest neighbour. And there was no light anywhere – it was so pitch, pitch black.

At times Will's mother was a bit awkward. She wasn't unkind to me, but she was a bit strict. I was more like a hired girl, there to do the housework. We had been told that a new house would be built for us on their farm when I arrived, but they changed their minds. The new house was built, but for Will's parents, and we were left with all the old junk, and I mean old junk. Will and I moved into the old house. We saved up eventually and built our own new one. I'm still in it, and I love it. I designed the new house, with plenty of room for all my entertaining. The sitting/dining room is sixteen by thirty feet.

I had left a fourteen-room house in Edinburgh. Pre-war, we had our own tennis court in the garden. Every year we had a tennis tournament. We had dances at the house every Saturday night all winter long, with an instructor and a dance mistress. After the dancing lessons, we ate and played cards until the wee hours of the morning. I brought my tennis racquet to Canada, but I never did get to use it. Eventually I gave it to a local auction.

I brought a lot of other items from home. A chair from my bedroom and a linen basket that matched. And a crystal dressing-table

A wife and son begin the long train journey to meet their "Canadian."

set that I still have. I brought two crystal butter dishes that my mother bought for me. One broke in my trunk, but I still have the other one and I use it every day. I also brought a solid silver tea urn on a stand, and I still use it, too.

I also have some sentimental things. My mum and dad gave me a gold chain and cross on the day I left home, and I wear it all the time. They also gave me a gold Mizpah ring that says, "Until death we do part," and I'm still wearing it. I also have my mother's Mizpah ring that she got from my dad when she married in 1898, but the saying has worn off completely.

I knew no one in Alberta, and I had no transport. I was so homesick that after eighteen months the doctor said, "You'd better go home. You're a walking skeleton." So I went back to England for three months and saw my family. I renewed my energy there and returned to Canada. My brothers never believed I'd make it in Canada. Nobody did. I decided I just had to make a go of it.

So I knuckled down and I learned to raise pigs (130 at a time) and deliver calves. I stooked a whole field while pushing my baby around in a buggy. We'd have at least twelve hired men coming in to help with the farm. We had to put them up and cook for them for during the harvest. How I did it, I don't know. Once, I was sent to get the cows. It was in the fall, and pitch-black in the valley where we lived. I walked up the hill with a lantern and I was fearful. My poor old heart was thumping away. All of a sudden, I saw animals in the darkness. I whacked one on its behind with a stick, but the animal didn't move. Why wouldn't it move? I looked underneath the animal and I knew there should be something that we pulled. I didn't know what an udder was called. I walked on and found another group and got on the ground with my lantern to check for something to pull on. They had udders, so I tapped one of the animals and I finally brought the cows to the barn. I went to the house with my heart thumping a thousand beats a minute!

One time, my husband was up in the bush and I had to water the cattle at the river. The river was frozen, but I wasn't tapping the ice, checking it, and all of a sudden I went through. I got out, but my boots were frozen on me, up to the knees by the time I got home. I sat on a chair in front of the old stove and put my frozen legs into the oven and kept them there until I could get my boots off. I learned to take a pole and to poke the ice ahead! The water sucks you straight under. I was lucky. I've had a guardian angel so many times. A friend said that I shouldn't really be here, I should really be six feet under, what with all the things that have happened to me since I came to Canada. It's amazing I'm still alive!

Having gone through such hard times makes you a much better person. Our first ten years on the farm were a disaster. We were buying the farm and had no money left after payments. We sold all our cattle and pigs, and just kept a cow for milk for the children and to make some butter. And some hens for eggs.

I cooked on a wood stove that made the kitchen hot in the summer. I put up at least four hundred jars every fall. We had no running water, we hauled it in, and I did the laundry on a scrub board until I had hardly any skin left on my hands. Back in Scotland, the washing at home went to the laundry! When I returned home that first time, I took a whole trunk of table linens to be washed by the laundry and properly ironed. I had never ironed a tablecloth in my life. On the farm we had old irons that had to be heated on the stove.

THAT'S WHAT I'M WAITING FOR!

Easy SPINDRY
WON'T WASTE YOUR SOAP AND HOT WATER

DO *All* YOUR WASHING JUST *Once* A WEEK!

You don't have to change your housekeeping routine to enjoy the washday freedom of modern EASY "Spindry"

It fits right into your home and your habits . . . Actually uses *less* hot water and soap than old-fashioned laundry methods . . . Requires no special built-in water and drain connections . . . Enables you to get all your washing out of the way just once a week . . . And really does *all* the work . . . Washes, rinses, dries, handles all water and launders *everything* from laces to blankets or comforters.

WHEN *can you get it?*

Naturally, you'll want to own this wonderful Easy Spindry Home Laundry . . . but it will be a little while yet before we can make deliveries. Better place your order *now*, with your EASY dealer.

The COMPLETE HOME LAUNDRY

WASHES clothes *clean*, by exclusive Vacuum-Cup Process, proved by test 50% to 75% easier on clothes.

RINSES and dries one tubful of clothes while a second full load is being washed. Automatic pump handles all water.

DRIES clothes *drier* in high-speed Rotary Spinner. Can't break buttons or damage fabrics. Dries blankets, comforters, sweaters, etc.

THE EASY WASHING MACHINE CO. LIMITED
TORONTO (10) ONTARIO

"That's what I'm waiting for!" says this advertisement.
Many brides waited a long time for such luxuries.

My dress-designing skills came in handy here. I made all my children's clothing and made my own until a few years ago. I still try to do a bit of knitting and embroidery.

By the second week of June, 1946, I joined the Farm Women's Group that met once a month at someone's home. That was the only connection I had with anybody. We met on the day nearest to the full moon so we would have light to travel at night. In the winter we went on a stoneboat. It was a really romantic trip with Will. The husbands went to the meeting – they met in another room.

There was no theatre, but Will and I went square dancing every night. We found it relaxing, even though we had to be up early the next morning for chores.

The second time I went back home, my first son was born over there. My mother was desperately ill, and the doctor said I'd go at my own risk, because my baby was due. So I went and I had my baby. I cared for Mum and the new baby. My dad lived for a long time after my mother died, and I went back thirteen times over the years. But I have no desire to go live there again.

My mother and father didn't visit me in Canada, but my brothers and sisters and other family members have visited. Until the late seventies, my sisters sent me linens, and seven times a year a twenty-pound box of chocolates and biscuits from Scotland because we couldn't afford them. They also sent clothing for the children and me. I don't know where we'd have been without family help. Nobody is sending things now. I'm the only one of my brothers and sisters left, and the only one left in the Ironside family, too.

Our house in Edinburgh has been partially demolished. The main part of the house is still there, as it's a heritage house. Little houses have been built in what was the garden, and the tennis court is now a great big cement parking lot that almost makes you cry to see it. My old bedroom and my parents' room are still there. I was invited in to see them on one of my visits. It's a shame to see your old home demolished.

I still live on the farm. It's now about a half section, all down to hay for the cattle. It used to be a bit of everything. I have some cattle and a big garden that I work in every day – it's a hobby for me that keeps me going. I have a hothouse for my tomatoes, just to give away to other people.

Though usually comfortable, a Canadian farm home is not luxurious. You have only one chance in five of having electric light . . . you have only eight chances in a hundred of finding any sort of plumbing in a farm, outside facilities taking its place.
— WELCOME TO WAR BRIDES

MARJORIE JAGGERS

I remember blackout, twenty-four war brides in a room on the *Rangitata*, lots of babies and children. We sailed around the Irish coast. It was the maiden voyage for this new ship. A convoy went with us, and it was quite an experience watching the ships signalling to each other.

The Salvation Army greeted us at Pier 21 and gave us oranges, apples, and bananas. My daughter Diana (eighteen months old, born during an air raid) was given a lovely crocheted dress. I was given Blue Ribbon Tea and a Magic Baking Powder cookbook, which I still use.

The porters on the train were wonderful. There were raffles on the train trip, and I won a cushion cover, black velvet with a deer on it. The tickets were one dollar.

We stopped in Winnipeg for twenty-four hours. We thought the women there were crazy, wearing long johns and fur coats, but we were the crazy ones. It was below zero. The men were from the mills and we thought they were convicts with their striped hats. We still laugh about it now!

We stopped in Jasper and I bought Diana a Raggedy Ann doll as big as she was.

I was going to Victoria, British Columbia, so I had to catch the ferry. I slept in a stateroom on the old boat. One other war bride came to Victoria with me.

I had a wonderful mother-in-law, but it was hard adjusting to the wood stove and the outdoor toilets. My husband started beating me. He always had a temper. I paid for him to go to barber school, but he wouldn't work. For a while he had a job as a mailman. He would pick up the mail and burn it later in our backyard. I bought some land and helped build our house. We had twelve acres. I worked many jobs: dug wells, cleaned septic tanks, washed dishes, ran a nursing home.

Our marriage never got better, so in 1960 I walked out with nothing. I got a job as Head of Servery at Government House. I had an office and staff. I served the Princess Royal, Princess Margaret, and Princess Alexandra. Princess Alexandra was wonderful. She arrived very late, and I had had a long day, setting up a buffet and setting the table. "You look tired," she told me. "We'll serve ourselves." And they did! And they put the dishes in the dumb waiter when they had finished! I loved that job.

------◆------

If you live on a farm near a town you will soon become acquainted with a great Canadian rural custom – Saturday night shopping. Everyone in the neighbourhood treks to town Saturday night, where they get their week's supplies and discuss the war news, politics and the state of the crops with their neighbours.

— WELCOME TO WAR BRIDES

------◆------

So few to do so much. The Pier 21 staff in 1946.

CAROLE LONG

I came from England on the *Scythia* in January 1953. I was in the WRAF and married Bill Long, one of the RCAF airmen stationed at Odiham. He was with the 421 Squadron, the first to go overseas after the war. We have never figured out why we came back by sea rather than by air.

My memories of Pier 21 are of the kind people. The Air Force Wing took care of me and the baby while Bill got all our trunks through. Then we were taken on a tour of Halifax, and, truthfully, I was not impressed. It was February 1, and there was lots of dirty snow. We were waiting for the train to Montreal, while Bill was to be stationed at Rockcliffe.

Bill's brother, sister-in-law, and mother met us in Montreal. I will never forget being jammed in the back seat of the car between these strangers. I had been told I should dress warmly, the baby too. I had so many clothes on, and they wouldn't let me take anything off. I think that is where I developed claustrophobia. I have to say that with the strange people, the heat, and what to me was a skating rink to drive on, it was the worst car ride I have ever had! Anyway, I am still here, loving Nova Scotia.

My daughter-in-law's father was a customs officer at Pier 21. We often wonder if he saw his future son-in-law when he was six months old!

One thing most British people like about Canada is the ease with which it is possible to get into open or wooded country from even the largest centres. Summer cottages are very popular.
— WELCOME TO WAR BRIDES

BETTY LOVITT

I married my husband, Lamont Lovitt, of the West Nova Scotia Regiment, on March 9, 1942. Our son was born to us on January 27, 1943, shortly before Lamont left England for the Sicilian and Italian campaigns. We did not see him again until the day we landed in Canada on June 15, 1945. He had returned to Canada on rotation leave via New York earlier in the year.

So we were reunited at Pier 21 the day we landed. The trip on the *Scythia* took nine days. There were twenty-eight mothers and twenty-eight children in the one long cabin, sleeping in double bunks. All of the children were under three years old, some were infants. Not your luxury cruise!

My husband was living in Dartmouth at the time, and we lived there for three months after my arrival. Then we moved to Port La Tour, our present address. We had four more children, three boys and two girls in all, and now have nine grandchildren and five great-grandchildren.

A trio of tired travellers.

JEANNIE (JENNY) MACKINNON

When the war broke out, I was in preparation for work at a children's sick-bay hospital. Like many children, my sisters and brother were evacuated to Maidenhead, but I stayed in London with my father. When the bombs got worse, my father told me to get a job in Maidenhead. Approximately three weeks after I left home, our house suffered a direct hit and my father was killed.

We were left orphans. At seventeen, I was the oldest, working at the hospital. When I became eighteen, I knew I would have to do "men's work." I had already received training from the London County Council Trade School, with a year in cookery and a year in sewing. I knew the forces would want me because of this training, but

I didn't want to go into the forces because I would have to leave my family.

I began working in a factory where we built Spitfires and Mosquitoes. After about six weeks' training, I began working on the rib cages of the training planes.

I got my calling-up papers, and so I went to the head of the factory, Mr. Peskin, and told him that I didn't want to go into the forces. The two of us went before a board, and Mr. Peskin told them that I didn't want to leave my family, I had received training, and I was very good at my job. The board gave me leave to stay on compassionate grounds and I worked at the factory until I was nineteen.

The part of the factory I didn't want to go into was called the "dope area." The fuselage of the planes was made of wood, and canvas was put over it. Then a kind of paint, "dope," was sprayed over it.

I was making five pounds a week at the factory, and I thought it was wonderful. In those days the pound was worth five dollars. However, after our house was destroyed, I did have to pay for lodgings. We wore overalls as a uniform, and those of us with long hair wore a heavy net called a snood. We worked from eight a.m. until five p.m., but during the Battle of Britain we worked overtime.

After one occasion of working late, Mr. Peskin treated us to supper. When we went outside, the fog was so thick we had to walk along the curb with one foot on the curb and the other in the gutter. We followed a bus whose conductor waved a lantern so the driver could see the road.

I remember my rations "for one person" – eight ounces of sugar, two ounces of butter a week, four ounces of cheese, one chop of meat a week and three slices of corned beef, two rashers of bacon, one egg every six weeks, and half a pint of milk every three days. We also got sausage, liver, or heart every six weeks. As well, I had points that I could use to buy flour and other items. I gave up putting sugar in my tea during the war, so I would have sugar for other things.

During this time, my brother and sisters were in school. They were billeted in homes and had families that loved them and they were very lucky. At the sick-bay hospital, there were many children who had been evacuated but had not been looked after properly. Many of the children there developed scabies.

For entertainment, I went to dances, or to the social centre in Slough. After paying sixpence, people could enjoy dances, roller-skating, or ice-skating for the month. People could also learn to knit or sew. We also went to the pictures.

One Saturday, I was going to visit a friend in Burnham. It was pouring rain, and I was on the bus. I became aware of a man in khaki standing behind me, and I became nervous and hoped he would get off before me, but no luck. He took my bag and said that he would carry it for me. I said no thank you, that I could carry it myself. However, once I looked into his kind face, I decided I was going to like him. His name was Archibald Alexander MacKinnon.

We made a date for the following Tuesday, and when the day arrived, I decided that I wasn't going to go. My landlady said I couldn't do that, that I had to go even if it was only to say that I wasn't going to stay. When I finally got there, almost an hour late, he was still waiting for me.

We dated for eight months, every night except Mondays. That was the night when I did my washing and ironing, washed my hair, got my rations, and did everything for the week. I was very fond of Archie, and I worried about going to Canada because I didn't really want to go. My family loved him, too. He somehow bought a football for my brother, which he still has.

Archie proposed to me in a field. He told me that I didn't have to worry, because we were going to get hitched. I told him that the only thing they hitched in England were the horses to the wagons!

I was twenty years old. Because I had no legal guardian and was under twenty-one, we had to go to court to get permission to be married. Archie was given a stern lecture there, because he was ten years older than I. We had to wait three months before we married.

I wanted a white wedding dress, but I wouldn't use my valuable clothing coupons for a dress I would only wear once. I was married in a pale blue dress with a royal-blue hat and shoes. I didn't want a second-hand ring or a utility wartime ring, so Archie's brother in America sent a new ring to us in a tobacco package. We were married August 5, 1944. When we came out of the church there was a group of men from the camp who had come to wish us well.

Archie soon left for France, before I even knew I was going to have a baby. When he received the news that his daughter Donna had been born, Archie's friend Percy jumped up on a table and yelled that Archie was a daddy! I was just twenty-one and the youngest mother in the ward.

My husband sailed for Canada six weeks before I did, in 1946. I sailed on the *Letitia* on August 1, arrived in Halifax on August 13, and was in North Sydney, Nova Scotia, on August 15. There were 400 wives and babies on the ship, and I was in the hold. There were no tubs to bathe in, so my friend Joyce and I took turns holding up coats so the other could wash with some privacy.

As we were coming into Halifax, I couldn't believe all the "Christmas trees" there were along the shore. I had never seen so many fir trees. Pier 21 just looked like a huge shed. Joyce looked after Donna while I looked for Archie. A newspaper photo was taken of me and four other war brides heading for Cape Breton.

Archie had spent the last three days trying to find somewhere for us to stay, but because we had a small child we couldn't find a place. Eventually, we went to the Salvation Army. The people there treated us kindly. (There was also a room full of war brides there who had been mistreated and were waiting to head back home to England.)

The next day, we started out by train for North Sydney. Breakfast was provided on the train, and the Salvation Army had provided a lunch for us. I remember the first station was called "Orangedale," a name I thought was unique.

Twenty-five war brides arrived in North Sydney, but at different times. Some had been there since 1943. There are ten of us who still get together. We found that in Cape Breton, the Scottish brides were more readily accepted than the English ones, while the reverse was

*"Civvies,"
or civilian
clothes, were
a new look
for many
couples, here
Mr. and Mrs.
Jack Wilson
of Toronto.*

true in Ontario. We were most surprised by the differences in expressions. My first Christmas, I was very lonely. In England, we played all kinds of games, but it wasn't done in my new home. I missed things like that dreadfully.

We had a difficult time. Archie had stayed in Europe for nine months after the war was over, and by the time he returned, it was hard for him to find a job. I didn't understand why Archie came back to Canada, because he had been offered a job with Ford Motorworks in England.

We built our home together, and after Archie found a job with Imperial Oil things became much easier.

---

*Only four Canadian children in every hundred go to private
schools, which are similar to British "public" schools.
The others go to elementary and secondary school, which are
maintained by public funds rather than fees.*
— WELCOME TO WAR BRIDES

DOROTHY MCILVEEN

On the morning of June 20, 1946, I boarded the train in Halifax, Yorkshire. I left Mum and Dad with sadness and apprehension, and yet with happy excitement. I was off to London. I soon met a fellow war bride, and we chummed together for the whole journey until we parted at Pier 21 in Halifax, Nova Scotia.

London was very hot, but the train ride to Southampton was pleasant. In Southampton, the huge ship *Aquitania* waited to carry us safely across the Atlantic to our new home in Canada. It was a beautiful evening as we pulled away from the dock. The seamen on an American warship anchored close by played tune after tune in farewell for us.

Finally, we lost sight of England. One girl, obviously Scottish, kept saying, "I'll never see bonnie Scotland again!" Each of us had our own thoughts, some sad, some quiet. Later, this all changed when we found where we had to sleep. I, along with the wives without children, were taken below, and there were row upon row of hammocks.

"What a hoot getting legged up at night!" The place was rocking with laughter. I had never been to camp or the YWCA. What an eye-opener I got, seeing all these girls in stages of dress and undress and no dress. I slept like a top.

Rolling out again in the morning was just about as much fun as getting in at night. The food on board was scrumptious, especially the fruit. Nevertheless, I found I could not eat much.

Before the war, Mum had bought a huge roll of crêpe de Chine, and I made cami-knicks, slips and bras, and nighties. They had lots of lace and looked quite dainty compared to our wartime undies. Mum suggested I throw away my old undies as I travelled so as to have all these beautiful undies when I arrived in Winnipeg. The girls developed a ritual for me each night – tossing Dorothy's old underwear out the porthole. What fun we had!

The evening of June 29, we anchored in Halifax Harbour. I remember there was a huge warehouse. I did not realize this was where I would be going the following morning. There was a girl dressed in white standing there, far below on the dock. I thought this was how they must dress in Canada. How fresh after our drab wartime clothes!

The following morning we were ushered onto Pier 21. It was a big place and noisy, and I must say I was happy when I had been processed and could leave. I crossed the train tracks to board a train going west. It was a very old train with Colonist coaches. The temperature was in the mid-eighties. There was no air conditioning, so the windows stayed open day and night. We were covered in soot. There was always a queue for girls to wash, not only hands and faces, but also hair. And generally, we wanted to cool down.

The trees and rocks seemed endless, and we were happy when we were allowed a few hours off the train in Ottawa. Unfortunately, a girl with appendicitis was taken to the hospital there.

The train stopped in Kenora, Ontario. Someone looked out and asked, "Who are these people?" The reply was, "They are Indians." All rushed to that side of the train. We were disappointed. They were not the Indians in our schoolbooks or in the movies. They were not warriors wearing feathers.

Soon, lots of girls had disembarked, and before much longer we rolled into Winnipeg. I thought, "This is it!" My husband, Mac, was waiting in a trilby hat and tweed suit. He had a smile a mile wide, and his parents were with him. The temperature was eighty-four, and I was cooking in my linen suit and stockings. My mother-in-law looked so cool in her pretty silk dress and floppy hat. (She was a lovely lady, and always kind to me.)

We arrived at Mac's home and had lunch. Then he had to go back to the office for a couple of hours. I couldn't wait to see the shops. I took the streetcar downtown – my first stop was the Bay. I was in sheer amazement at all the beautiful things. I went crazy, buying Coty perfume, lipstick, stockings, and new bras. As for the bras, I was tired of making my own from scraps, looking like two fried eggs. Now I would have points like the Canadian girls.

As I strolled down Portage Avenue, I spotted a white dress with blue cornflowers. I tried on the dress and bought it. It was a size nine and a bit baggy, but I could fix that. A few stores along, I bought blue

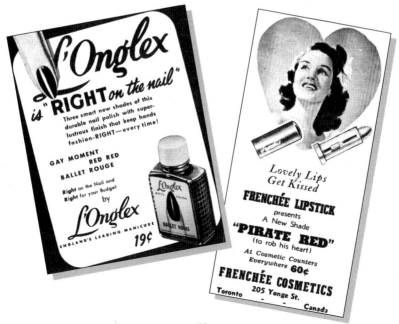

linen shoes to match the dress. I was really on a roll, and I hadn't even reached Eaton's yet! At Eaton's, I tried on a beaver coat, so soft and elegant. (I only tried it on.) I was catching on to the currency, even though I was mumbling to myself in pounds, shillings, and pence. I continued on my buying spree. When I returned to my mother-in-law's house, she opened the door and howled with laughter when she saw all the parcels.

On my first Saturday, Mac and I and four couples took the moonlight train to Winnipeg Beach to stay at the family cottage for the weekend. As the only married couple, Mac and I were given the duty of buying the weekend food. Each couple chipped in five dollars, I remember, which covered the food and the beer. The only stores I had been in were the ones in Winnipeg on my first day. We bought bread, milk, eggs, bacon, and so on. At the meat counter, the butcher had a huge platter of wiggly-looking meat. Mac bought two pounds, and I asked what it was, and he said it was for burgers. "Oh yes, what are burgers?" I wondered. I bought sausages. The burgers were made and barbecued for dinner and were delicious. I couldn't believe that awful stuff could turn out so good.

In the evening, we went to the Beach dance in a huge hall with walls of wood halfway up and screening at the top. How strange! I was the only girl in a dress. It was my new white one with the blue cornflowers. Midnight saw us swimming in the lake, and there was a late-night dance at a small fishing village on Lake Winnipeg. All the band members were tipsy, drinking something out of sealer jars. Wow, this was really wild!

The sun had risen as we rode back to the cottage and rolled into our beds. At eight o'clock in the morning, Jim, with a booming voice, was calling, "Hit the deck! Breakfast is on." As we made our way through the kitchen, Betty was screwing up her face and shaking her beautifully manicured hands, saying, "Wieners! Wieners! For *breakfast*!"

I said to Mac, "What's wrong with her?" He laughed, saying, "Oh, Dorothy, you bought wieners instead of sausages!"

IF YOU THINK THIS IS FUNNY

Have you ever rode the briny deep
While the Atlantic rollers dip and creep?

And one clambers over the other side,
And the ship is full of Canadian war brides?

And the cabin baggage is not all there,
And the girls come in and pull your hair?

And the passengers weep and the babies bawl,
And some say they don't want to sail at all?

And some want a lower instead of an upper,
And the first sitting for dinner and second for supper?

And the wind without warning begins to rise,
And the waves rear up to a stupendous size?

And the mothers are sick and the babies not,
And the nurses want to drown the lot?

And the stewards go around with a mop and pail,
And wind has now become a gale?

And the soldiers' arms are full of babies,
And the nursery sounds like pups with rabies?

And the skipper over the mike shouts out,
"We've engine trouble!" and turns about?

And the ship turns back to Britain's shore,
And the brides say, "Please, no more, no more!"?

'Cause if you think this is funny and want to laugh,
We'll sign you up as one of the staff!

[author unknown, written circa 1946]

I answered, "Well, I thought they looked rather severe." We still laugh about it.

The year that followed saw us living in Brandon, Manitoba, where our oldest son, Tim, was born. Then we moved to Winnipeg, where our daughter, Margaret, and younger son, David, were born. We spent years in Regina, Saskatchewan, then went back to Winnipeg, and finally moved to Victoria on Vancouver Island, where Mac and I have celebrated more than fifty-five years of marriage.

Canada is a big, beautiful country. My life here has been truly happy. Our dear family, four healthy grandchildren, and wonderful friends have made it that way.

Some of the British brides already in Canada have found themselves buying all the things they hadn't seen for months, and not having enough money left for the rent.
— WELCOME TO WAR BRIDES

PATRICIA MCKINLEY

I married a Canadian soldier in Aldershot, Hampshire, in 1946 and came alone to Canada on the *Letitia* that same year, a month before my husband. There was a really nice panelled library for our use on the ship, and in the evenings we played bingo. I think the things that really impressed me the most upon arriving in Canada were the vastness of the country, the houses mostly built of wood, the amount of snow on the ground in Quebec, and the availability of food. I still remember the first banana I'd seen since 1939, seven years before.

Alfred Nash of Toronto offers his wife, Margaret, a plate of bananas – the ultimate treat!

ELSIE MILLS

I stood at the window today, looking across a field of sweet corn. So many years have passed and so much has happened. The sun is shining and the sky looks so huge. That was my first impression of Canada, on May 25, 1945.

I was the sixth of ten children. I began working in a hospital in London and had chosen nursing for a career. My father, having moved out of Admiralty headquarters in London, was relocated to the Pump Room Hotel in Bath, which was turned into offices for the duration of the war. My father moved my mother and younger family members to Bristol, so I moved to Fishponds Hospital in Bristol to be close to them.

Bombs dropped frequently, and air-raid sirens went every night. Women were being called up to join the services. I was in a reserved job, but decided to join the air force as a WAAF (Women's Auxiliary Air Force) and took a job training as a dental clerk orderly. I was posted to Paignton, Devon, and the fickle finger of fate stirred the pot. My Canadian husband-to-be was in a convalescent hospital in Brixham, Devon, about ten miles from Paignton. I was on duty the night we met, and wasn't supposed to be at a dance, but I was! Ed was with a group that had come over to the dance. He ran out of money to get back, so I staked him a taxi fare. I always told him I just married him to make sure he paid me back, and I still say he didn't!

Life with Ed was always interesting. He rejoined the army in 1948 and served until 1968. We lived in Ontario, Quebec, back to Ontario, Germany, and Manitoba. Ed served in Holland and England during the war, and Cyprus, Korea, and Germany as a peacekeeper. I found life very busy, but with Ed's frequent absences, I was lonely.

I have lived in all shapes and sizes of houses. The smallest was at Wasaga Beach, Ontario, when Ed came back from Korea. It was so small that the bedrooms held only a bed and dresser, and we had to crawl over the bed to get into the room. There was a river running along the bottom of the property, and our son Ian used to sweet-talk the fishermen out of a fish almost every week. That house was a lot better, though, than the H-hut we lived in at Wolseley Barracks in London, Ontario. We really had to watch out for rats coming up the standing pipe.

In 1949, army pay was really poor and good homes hard to find. Polio was a constant summertime threat, and bulbar polio visited us. Our eldest daughter, Betty, was one sick lass, but she was tough and she survived, and off we went to Montreal. There, we lived above a restaurant. The kids loved it and visited downstairs frequently.

In Germany, we lived above a butcher shop and saw some strange ways of curing meat. I have never really enjoyed hot dogs since. We moved to PMQs (permanent married quarters) in Soest and Werl, Germany. They were really nice three-bedroom, beautifully furnished apartments. We moved to Winnipeg, Manitoba, and our furniture, after four years in storage, finally arrived, smelling bad. It seems there had been a flood while we were away. The army doesn't believe in compensation, and you sign papers that say you won't talk to the media, so, like a good soldier, you accept life and get on with it.

We moved into a little house in Winnipeg PMQs. During the winter, the upstairs bedroom wall would freeze and with it, any sheet or blanket that touched it. How cold does it get in Winnipeg? Answer: so cold that if you hang washing on the line, it snaps right off, leaving the pegs and anything attached – hems, toes of socks – hanging there until spring.

In 1968, Ed was sick, so, having completed twenty-six years of active service, he decided to retire from the army. We came back to London, Ontario, to be close to his family.

My mother died in 1953 while we were stationed in Montreal, and my father died in 1955 while we were at Camp Borden, Ontario. I had the opportunity to return to England with my children in 1958, on the way to join my husband in Germany. Although I wasn't able to see my parents again, I visited with the rest of my family.

In Halifax, there is a reminder of my father's expertise. The admiralty anchor that is on the corvette was the anchor modified by my father. Anchors at one time used to be pulled up by hawser and put on the deck. My father, Alfred Nash, modified it to allow it to slide up the outside of the ship and lock into the side. The first of these anchors were put on an Indian line of ships in 1936.

What a shock it was for me to come from a home that was planned and built by my father to live in a terrace house with a pump in the well for water and a loo down the garden. The snow in the winter was pushed back to the hydro wires and the doctor travelled on snowshoes to visit his patients. Emergency items and yeast to make bread were dropped by parachute until the snow could be blasted and the trains could get through during one difficult winter. I wanted to go home – but I didn't. The girls the Canadian soldiers brought home as brides were tough, but then we had endured more than five years of war, hadn't we?

●

It seems that many Canadians would rather sleep ten minutes
longer in the morning than take time to eat a proper breakfast.
You may rightly take a dim view of this misguided habit –
so do we! Lots of Canadians do eat good breakfasts though
and these are the ones we are interested in.
— CANADIAN COOK BOOK FOR BRITISH BRIDES

●

OLIVE MINNINGS

I met Al at a Friday-night dance. I sneaked out with my girlfriend, whose sister was a nurse and had access to a vehicle. I told my dad I was staying overnight with my girlfriend, but I was going to dance with a young man I'd met.

I was showing off while dancing, with my pleated skirt to just above my knees, and I saw Al across the room. I thought, "What nice teeth he has!" He was sitting with another fellow, and they were watching us dance. I liked his teeth and he liked my legs! My date had to leave the dance early, and at the coffee break Al came over and told me he couldn't dance but he'd like to take me to supper. My original date later came back and asked me to jitterbug – we were the only two doing it. Later, I found out that Al had said to his friend, "See that girl? I'm gonna marry that girl." That was before we even spoke to each other!

He visited me at home a few times, and we went to the movies, then he went off to war. I was engaged to an English fellow and broke off with him. That same night, I got a letter from Al saying he could visit on his next leave.

The first time he asked me to marry him, I said no. Another time, he said he had to go back to Canada, but he wouldn't have to go if he were married. So I said, "Why don't we get married?" I get teased that I proposed to Al!

We married on August 22, 1946. I was given silver horseshoes when I left the church, and a rolling pin and a wooden spoon. The pin and spoon were supposed to bring you luck as a good cook. They

weren't to use to plonk your husband! I still have the spoon, and I have always used it to cook jam. I used the rolling pin as a hammer, but I never used it on Al!

Al headed to Canada in October, and I left England on the *Letitia*, which used to be called the *Empire Brent*. Our first boarding at Liverpool was November 24, 1946, but in the early morning, after leaving the dock, the ship ran into a cattle boat in the Mersey and the cattle boat capsized. Imagine the confusion when it was announced we would be sent back home, or to a hostel in London, while repairs were made. We would be advised when to return. Newspapers reported war brides hanging over the sides of the ship crying out in horror. That was not entirely true, because at five a.m., when it happened, most of us were in bed.

After the ship was repaired, we left England a second time, on December 4. Things got confused when I got to the ship late and sent Al a telegram so he'd expect me at a different time. The telegram he got said, "Not coming. Don't worry. Love Olive." The telegraph office had shortened the message, so Al got the wrong idea and thought I wasn't coming at all.

Cattle Ship Sinks In Collision But No Human Lives Lost

LIVERPOOL, Nov. 20—(CP Cable)—No human lives were lost today when the bride-ship Empire Brent, carrying 900 wives and children of Canadian servicemen to Halifax, capsized the cattle steamship Stormont in an early morning collision in the foggy Mersey.

The Empire Brent is better known to Canadians as the former hospital ship Letitia.

(The Canadian Wives Bureau in London said that none of the _____'s passengers was hurt. A statement will b____

It was a rough eight-day crossing, three days longer than the average fine-weather crossing of the time. For two of those days, we were held outside Halifax Harbour because it was too rough to dock. When we finally disembarked, the temperatures were well below any we had ever experienced and we were unprepared. Our light clothing was little comfort as we stood waiting for our luggage, which in those days was sorted outside or in unheated sheds.

My husband's parents had moved from Lanigan, Saskatchewan, where my husband was born, to Victoria during the war. The brides heading for British Columbia were in the first of twenty train carriages leaving Halifax when we arrived there. By the time we got to Calgary, there was only one carriage left, ours, and it was hooked to the back of a regular train. When we arrived in Vancouver, our car was way at the end. We couldn't see our husbands and they couldn't see us. When I didn't see Al, I thought, "I'll go to the Red Cross and go home!" The Red Cross would pay your fare back to Britain if you stayed in Canada six months and were still unhappy.

Then I saw Al, in a trilby hat and a loud plaid jacket. Eventually I got rid of his hat and jacket! On December 21, I was in Victoria with Al, and we've been there ever since.

In the limited space [of this booklet] it has been impossible to give details but your husband's descriptive ability has probably enabled him to fill in the gaps.
— WELCOME TO WAR BRIDES

MURIEL (MICKI) MORE

My roots are dear, and I am still able to visit my homeland, Edinburgh, Scotland, but I am now a Canadian and proud to be in the finest country.

I met my husband, George, in London. I was a dancer in a musical in 1939. My company gave a party for the RCAF squadron George was in. We corresponded during the war. I joined up as a leading airwoman, "Sparks" as we were called, after the London Blitz, when the theatres were closed temporarily. I put on shows for the troops while I had my wireless job.

When the war was over, and George had two weeks until he went home to Canada, we had a great reunion and he proposed marriage.

My parents loved him. He applied to be married at his repatriation station, and he was made a ship's officer. The troops weren't going out for eight weeks.

We were married on a windy day, April 4, 1946, in the Edinburgh church I was christened in. My husband's co-pilot was his best man. My attendants (just a niece and cousins) and I were anchoring my train. I handed my bouquet to my husband, and one of the newspaper photographers got the picture. It was printed in the paper with the caption "Guess Who Is the Ballet Dancer?" because George was standing in a near-perfect third position.

After my husband returned to Canada, I arrived two months later on the *Aquitania* in September 1946. There was a marvellous train trip from Halifax to Winnipeg. An officer would tell us who would be meeting us at our stops. It was interesting, seeing the reception for the brides who got off at the stops along the way. There were nervous husbands holding corsages. Some shy Scottish lassies were saying, "If my Johnny has flowers, I'm nae gettin' off the train," and others said, "My man better have some flowers!"

When I arrived in Winnipeg, George's Scottish parents were waiting outside the platform gate. With shaking hands, they pinned a corsage of sweetheart roses on me. I stayed with George's parents, and they took me shopping for a parka and warm clothes before I went east to Sioux Lookout, Ontario. My husband and his former navigator had bought a fishing and hunting resort from some friends who were retiring from the business.

There were two lodges: the main inn, where we would reside, and another building we called the far lodge, eight miles up the Little Vermilion Lake, that our partner and his English bride managed. Our first winter in Sioux it was fifty-six degrees below zero. I didn't feel the cold – I was from Edinburgh. My husband taught me how to ski, and I was in love. Such happiness there, and, oh, those sunsets! Our beautiful son was born there in 1948.

We later lived in Toronto, where I had a dancing school for seventeen years. My dashing Canadian pilot-husband, George, died in 1985, and I have since moved to Vancouver, British Columbia. I recently retired from teaching dance. I am so happy to be a Canadian.

───────────●───────────

If you make friends wherever you go, you are not only doing
a fine job for yourself but you are also acting as an unofficial
ambassador in helping to cement further that good will which
exists between our two countries.

– WELCOME TO WAR BRIDES

───────────●───────────

PHYLLIS OLIVER

I arrived in Halifax on the *Duchess of Bedford*, on May 27, 1945, and was guided to the train. En route to Saskatoon, Saskatchewan, the train stopped, and it was a wonderful experience to be greeted by the local residents, who supplied us with fruit, chocolate bars, and cigarettes. They, of course, were interested to hear which areas in England we came from.

On a rainy afternoon, we arrived in Montreal and stopped for a few hours. I had met a young Canadian woman on the train, and she asked me if I would like to go into the city. I accepted her offer, as I was anxious to purchase a pair of shoes. She took me to Eaton's and helped me (my French wasn't that good) select a pair of dress shoes.

Back on the train, I was feeling a little more relaxed – the homesick yearning was wearing off, and I was looking forward to joining my husband, John, in Saskatoon. I had read and been told about the vast expanse of flat land in the Prairies, but it was still overwhelming. I realized then that I would be a great distance from the Atlantic or Pacific ocean, and I would miss the sea and the beaches. I would also

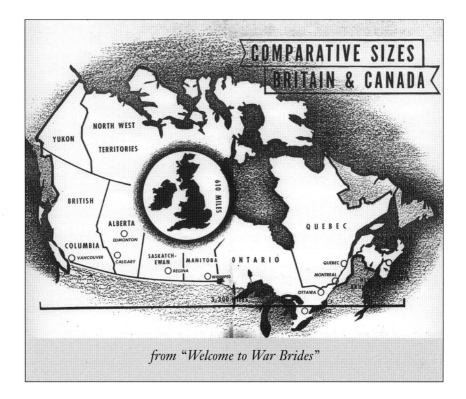

from "Welcome to War Brides"

miss the forest, where I had always enjoyed walking and listening to the birds.

The journey to Saskatoon seemed endless. At 10 p.m., the train pulled to a stop in Saskatoon, and I was escorted by the Red Cross hostess to where my husband and his mother were waiting to greet me. We stayed with my mother-in-law for two months, and then purchased our home on the same road. I have lived in Saskatoon ever since.

I have made several trips back to England. After my father's death, my eighty-seven-year-old mother came to Saskatoon to live with John and me. Relatives and friends were very kind to her. She had wonderful health, enjoyed travelling with us to Eastern and Western Canada, and had a wonderful celebration for her 100th birthday. She lived to be 102.

Canada is my home, and the years have been filled with much joy. However, I still love the British comedies and films, and British humour. I have many cherished memories of the land of my birth.

Dessert – Pie must be mentioned first, for it is undoubtedly Canada's favourite dessert. . . . If you ask your husband what he'd like for dessert, his answer will probably be "Anything, as long as it's pie!"
– CANADIAN COOK BOOK FOR BRITISH BRIDES

MARGERY PAIGE

I met my husband, "Blackie" Paige, in London in 1942. We married the following year, and our daughter Arlene was born in 1944. After being overseas for five-and-a-half years, Blackie yearned to return to Canada. Though I have never regretted his decision, and love this country, I must admit at the time I would have loved to stay in England.

I sailed on the *Franconia* on March 29, 1945. When we wondered why it was taking thirteen days to cross, we were told we had sailed south to the Azores in order to avoid enemy submarines and mines.

We docked at Pier 21 early on the morning of April 11. I had gone on deck to see what all the commotion was about. To the left, I noticed rows of white wooden houses, all with coloured roofs of red, blue, and green. I thought it looked just like a fairyland, with all the lights on! What a contrast it was to London, which was still in a blackout when we left and had houses built of brick with grey roof tiles. I thought, "I'm really going to like this place, with all these lights and houses with coloured roofs."

During the voyage, we had taken some classes to learn about Canadian money, clothes, the climate, and so on, and I remember the rate of exchange was $4.44 to the pound.

After disembarking, we all sat on the quayside with our one suitcase each. It seemed as though the arrangements were made according

LOSSARY

English	Canadian	English	Canadian
Bank holiday	Legal holiday	Ladder	Run
Banknote	Bill	(in stocking)	
Basin	Mixing Bowl	Larder	Pantry
Beer or "Bitter"	Ale or beer	Lavatory	Toilet
Biscuit, sweet	Cookie	Lift	Elevator
unsweetened		Lounge suit	Business suit
Bill (in a	Check	Lorry	Truck
restaurant)		Luggage	Baggage
Block of Flats	Apartment house	Macintosh	Raincoat
Boiled Sweets	Candy (hard)	Made-to-order	Tailor made
Book a table	Reserve a place	Maize—	Corn
Book passage	Get Tickets	Indian corn	
Booking Office	Ticket Office	Motorcar	Automobile
Braces	Suspenders	Multiple stores	Chain Stores
Bureau	Writing desk or	Napkins (baby's)	Diapers
	Secretary	Paraffin	Coal oil
Cab rank	Taxi stand	Pavement	Sidewalk
Caretaker	Janitor	Petrol	Gasoline
Chemist	Druggist	Plate	Silverware
Chemist's shop	Drug Store	Plum cake	Fruit cake
Chest of drawers	Bureau	Pillar box	Mail box
(low)		Post (of a letter)	Mail
Cinema	Movies	Potato crisps	Potato chips
Corn	Grain	Pram	Baby carriage
Cotton wool	Absorbent cotton	Pullover	Sweater
Corset	Girdle	Reel of cotton	Spool of thread
Court shoes	Pumps	Return	Round trip
Cupboard	Closet	Rubber	Eraser
Curtains	Drapes	Scent	Perfume
Dickey	Rumble seat	Shooting	Hunting
Draper's shop	Dry Goods Store	Shopwalker	Floorwalker
Dress circle	Balcony	Silencer	Muffler
Dressing table	Dresser	(motor car)	
Dustbin	Garbage can	Single (ticket)	One way
Dustman	Garbage man	Sledge	Sled
Face flannel	Wash rag,	Spanner	Wrench
	wash cloth	Spirits	Liquor
First floor	Second floor	Stalls	Orchestra seats
Fishmonger	Fish dealer	Steadings	Farm buildings
Flat	Apartment	Stores	Groceries
	(or Flat)	(household)	
Frying pan	Skillet, frying pan	Suspenders	Garters
	or spider	Sweets	Candy
Galoshes	Rubbers	Sweet or savoury	Dessert
Gangway	Aisle	Tart	Pie
(theatre)		Teats	Nipples
Geyser	Water heater	Threepenny and	Five and Ten Store
Goods van, truck	Freight car	Sixpenny Bazaar	
Gramophone	Phonograph	Tinned	Canned
Greengrocery	Grocery store	Torch	Flashlight
Grilled	Broiled	Tram, tramway	Streetcar
Ground floor	First floor	Treacle	Molasses or syrup
Guard	Conductor or	Trunk call	Long distance
	brakeman	Tube	Subway
Haberdashery	Men's Wear	Undercut	Tenderloin
High boots	Boots	(of beef)	
High Street	Main Street	Upper circle	Second balcony
Hire purchase	Instalment plan	Valve (wireless)	Tube
Hoarding	Bill Board	Waistcoat	Vest
Ices	Ice Cream	Washing	Laundry
Ironmongery	Hardware Store	Wellingtons	Rubber boots
Joint	Roast	Wireless	Radio
Jug	Pitcher	Van	Truck
		Vest	Undershirt

from "Welcome to War Brides"

to the alphabet, which meant most of the women were allowed to board the train ahead of me. It was parked alongside the quay. When the P's were called, I couldn't wait, as the other women were already eating their lunch and holding their plates up to us along the quay. We saw steak, white rolls, and ice cream. However, when my food came, I couldn't help but think of England, and how this meat I had on my plate would have been the ration for our family of five for one week.

When the train stopped in Lévis, Quebec, Arlene and I were taken off. Arlene was so sick with dysentery we were taken to a Red Cross nursing station so that a doctor could look at her. The nurses were marvellous and told me to go for a walk and see something of Lévis. I did not venture very far, because I could not speak French, and I hadn't had any previous dealing with the money, but I do remember seeing a bunch of bananas hanging in a shop window. I remember thinking, if only I could send my mother a couple of them. After a day or so on the train, I kept thinking my mother would never be able to find me. In England, if you travelled on a train for a whole day, you would be in the ocean! The scenery was terrific, just like the postcards we had seen of Canada, with the Christmas trees everywhere.

My husband's sisters welcomed me with open arms. I remember going to downtown Melfort a few days after arriving and being treated to a banana split. I so enjoyed it, and kept remarking how marvellous it was to get bananas and ice cream again! Blackie's nephew, who was about sixteen, bought me another banana split. It was very kind of him, but I just could not eat it, so he did.

During my first three months in Canada, I stayed with my husband's parents on their farm in Lennoxville, Quebec. Eggs, butter, and milk were plentiful, and I learned how to make wonderful angel food cakes, cookies, desserts, and such. When I went back to England in 1948 for a visit, I told my mother all about these lovely ten-inch-high angel food cakes and promised to bake one for her. When I told her I needed ten eggs, my mother replied, "What!" Even in 1948, food was still rationed – one egg per person per month.

Needless to say, she never tasted an angel food cake until she came to Canada in 1958.

When I first arrived via train in Melfort, Saskatchewan, it was 7:30 a.m. Blackie, who was back with the Royal Canadian Mounted Police, had just completed the night shift and was wearing his RCMP uniform when he met us at the station. Until this point, I had only seen him dressed in his army uniform. There he was in his navy britches with wide yellow stripes down each side, and a cap with a shiny peak. I said, "Oh, do you play in a band?" I don't think my comment was appreciated!

In Melfort, we stayed at the Winston Hotel for three days while we went furniture shopping. My husband had managed to rent an apartment over Bush's Garage. We moved in on a Friday and unpacked our dishes and put the cardboard box with the straw in it on the back porch at the top of the stairs. I had never used a wood stove before, so I emptied the ashes from the grate into the empty cardboard box. I thought that the ashes were harmless because they were grey. However, as you might guess, a fire started, and we were lucky to get out down the stairs. The fire engine came, and Arlene and I were taken to another apartment nearby. When my husband came home, expecting his lunch prepared, he was directed to us, and as he came through the door, I shouted, *"I want to go home, right now!"* My husband replied, "If you start any more fires, you will go home."

On the way back to the hotel after the fire, a woman stopped us in the street and asked, "Are you the English war bride who has just had a fire?" When I replied yes, she said, "I would be very happy if you would come and stay with me, as I have a spare room." We thanked her and declined, but I was very moved by this. Although we lived in Melfort for three years, I never did find out who the woman was.

We had to live in the hotel for three weeks while the apartment was painted and the stairs replaced. When my husband went to the desk to pay our bill, the clerk told him, "It has all been taken care of. The Legion has paid your account." Such an abundance of kind gestures awaited me in Canada.

Because Blackie was in the RCMP, we lived in many small towns and villages in northern Saskatchewan, and in the Peace River area of Alberta. We also lived for a time in Regina, and finally retired to Edmonton. I am very fortunate to be living in this wonderful country, and I will be forever grateful to Blackie for not listening to me when I wanted to stay in England.

Afternoon Tea is a treat – not a daily routine – probably because the Evening Meal is served so early, usually around 6 o'clock.
— CANADIAN COOK BOOK FOR BRITISH BRIDES

JEANNE PERRY

In 1942, I had planned to stay in Birmingham for Christmas. My friends and I had been asked to help at the Men's Service Club, and we volunteered to work around midnight. A group of Canadian Air Force men came in. One of them was Lance Corporal Allan Perry. He was on a training course near Birmingham. He asked me for coffee, and I later agreed to go to a dance with him. We met frequently and became engaged at Caswell Bay on the Gower Coast in 1943. By this time, I had joined the WAAF and was sweeping the floors of the hangars. It was a job that never ended!

Allan and I were married on January 1, 1944, in St. Cynog's Church at Ystradgynlais, South Wales. Our honeymoon was spent at Stratford-upon-Avon, England. We returned to our stations and continued to meet as often as possible. I became pregnant and was discharged from the WAAF. I joined Allan at his station in Bath, England, and again at Winkle, a small place in Devon. When Allan was sent to Margate, I returned to my home at Ystradgynlais. Our daughter

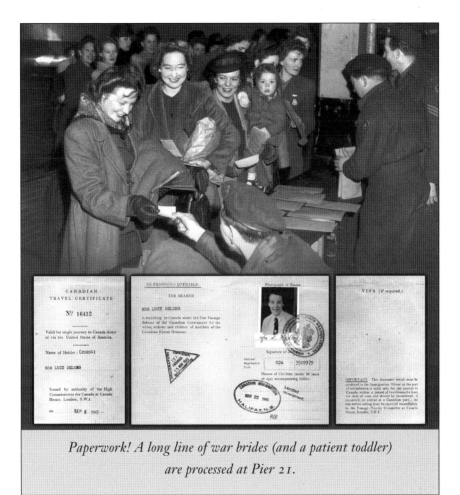

*Paperwork! A long line of war brides (and a patient toddler)
are processed at Pier 21.*

Sheila was born on March 12, 1945. Allan saw us at the hospital and
once at Ystradgynlais before he returned to Canada later in the year.

On April 3, 1946, I landed in Halifax, at Pier 21, aboard the
Letitia. The military personnel there checked my papers and
informed me of the importance of my Canadian Travel Certificate.
They explained that it was my proof of being a Canadian citizen. I
have kept it safe ever since.

Before we boarded a train that would take a "northern route," a
Canadian volunteer met us. The woman was a lovely person. She told
me that Sheila looked cold in her short coat, and she gave me a blue
snowsuit with white fur around the hood, and a bag of toiletries for

the baby and me. Sheila was ill at the time, so the woman also got some medicine for her.

The "northern route" was bush country, and where the snow had melted I saw black dirt roads. Winnipeg was the largest city we came to, and Allan's brother Jim attended university there. He came to see us when we stopped at the station. Sheila and I travelled on to Regina. Allan was there, his arms went around us both. It felt so good. It was wonderful to be together again. We got to the hotel, left our luggage, and took Sheila to see Dr. Brown. He told us not to move from the hotel for three days. Allan stayed with the baby while a family friend took me to Simpson's department store.

What an awe-inspiring store it was to someone from the war-torn British Isles. Gorgeous dresses – and the makeup! Wow! There were no crowded lineups of people waiting to be served.

Eventually, Allan, Sheila, and I travelled to Estevan. It was so good to be at the end of the journey. Although the Perry family was great to me, that first year was difficult. I was homesick and felt that I did not belong to the community. I followed the advice of a friend who told me that to belong to a community one has to become a volunteer within it. This I did, and still do.

My sister Mary and her family immigrated to Estevan in 1966. My parents came for a year's holiday – and the following year they also immigrated to Estevan. This was a bonus for me!

I have been fortunate and have returned home many times. Allan and I have four children, twelve grandchildren, and one great-grandchild. All have done excellently well, and we both love them all.

Feathery light steamed and baked puddings are liked in cold weather but suet pudding you would be wise to avoid unless your man has acquired a taste for it overseas.
– CANADIAN COOK BOOK FOR BRITISH BRIDES

*Canadians are informal people, and will never criticize
you for what you haven't got.*
— CANADIAN COOK BOOK FOR BRITISH BRIDES

JOAN PETERSON

I arrived on the *Mauretania* on March 6, 1946, as a twenty-two-year-old war bride with my two-year-old daughter.

We had to travel by train to Shelburne, Nova Scotia, at seven o'clock in the morning. The other passengers on the train were very friendly, and by the time we arrived in Shelburne I had a recipe for making a pound of butter stretch to two, a recipe for war cake, and a bag of apples, oranges, and chocolate bars.

My husband, Sherburne, "Sherb" for short, was waiting for us in Shelburne, and we went by taxi to his home six miles outside of town. The road wasn't paved and was very muddy due to the spring thaw. The taxi got mired in the mud and my husband had to go to the nearest home and get someone with a team of oxen to haul us through.

I had never seen oxen before and wondered what kind of place I had come to! We stayed with my husband's mother for two months, and then moved to Yarmouth and into a home of our own. We have lived in this house for over fifty years, and raised seven children.

FLORENCE PHILLIPS

My story begins in 1938, when my future husband decided to go to England to play hockey.

*Florrie
and Scoop,
after one
year and
three months
of marriage.*

I met him in 1939 on a Saturday night at the Forest Gate Roller Skating Rink. I usually went with a friend, but this Saturday she was unable to go, so I took the train from London Fields and went on my own. As I was skating around, this chap with a funny accent came up and spoke to me. That's how it all started.

He introduced himself as "Scoop." I thought, That's an odd name. Apparently his mother had nicknamed him after a cartoon character in a Winnipeg newspaper. His birth name was Percy, but in later years he acquired another nickname, Phil, which most of his friends called him.

We corresponded and met when we could. He was working at Dagenham then, as a welder.

I remember when war was declared: September 3, 1939, my mum's birthday. The air-raid sirens went off and we all dashed into our Anderson shelter in the back garden in London. Thank goodness the all-clear went a couple of hours later. It was very scary, being the first air raid we'd heard.

Then came the Blitz in 1940. My parents stayed in London all through it. I remember my dad taking his time doing up his shoelaces and getting his tin hat. The bombs were dropping, and I'd say, "Hurry up, Dad, and get in the shelter."

Scoop and I were married in London on July 20, 1940. We had a simple wedding. The only flowers I could get for my bouquet were cornflowers. We had a great party afterwards, at my parents' home. My cousin was the pianist in a band. They played "In the Mood" many times during the evening.

We went to live in Ruislip, as Scoop worked in Northolt and then Farnborough. In April 1941, he enlisted in the Canadian Army in London. I then had to do a wartime job. I nearly joined the Land Army, and then changed my mind when a government job became available with the War Risks Insurance.

We were evacuated to a big mansion near Ascot. I shared a room with three other girls. A jolly bunch. We all got on so well together.

There were forty-three on the staff. We used to go to dances in the village hall in Sunningdale. There were some Americans, but mostly Canadians. My husband would come from Aldershot and stay some weekends. I would also go and visit my parents in London.

One of my friends I worked with lived in Windsor Great Park, at one of the lodges. Her husband was a gamekeeper in the park. When I was expecting my first son, she asked me if I would like to go and stay there, which I did. Anyone who lived in the park was able to be christened at the Royal Chapel, a dear little chapel. My son Raymond arrived in March 1944 and was christened there.

When the war ended, Scoop came back to Canada. I went to stay in London with my parents until I left for Canada. I sailed on the *Queen Mary*, leaving Southampton June 10 and arriving at Pier 21 on June 15, 1946. It was heartbreaking leaving my parents, as I was an only child. Prime Minister Mackenzie King was on our ship. Later, during our railway trip, we got out for a stretch and Mr. King patted my son on the head and said, "Hello, Sonny."

I broke my journey to visit my mother's sister and her family in Hamilton, Ontario. She came out to Canada in 1912. She had broken up with her English boyfriend. In the meantime, he immigrated to Canada with his family. When he got settled in a job, he sent my aunt a ring and asked her to come out to Canada and get married, which she did. How romantic! She never returned to England. It was a big event for me to meet my Canadian cousins. They made such a fuss of me.

What a journey crossing Canada by train! Such lovely scenery, especially when we came through the Rockies.

I was met in Vancouver by my brother-in-law. Then I was on my way to my in-laws in Victoria. I stayed with them for six months. Scoop would get over from Vancouver to visit every second weekend. I was very homesick and not very happy in Victoria. I decided to go over to Vancouver and look for a place to stay.

We lived at a motel for a couple of weeks, and then we were able to get a room in the old Hotel Vancouver. The veterans were staying in the hotel with their families.

The house we were having built was ready in August 1947. Our second son, Graham, was three weeks old when we moved in. In 1953, my parents decided to immigrate to Canada. That made me very happy. Mum and Dad took a big chance in finding employment at their age. They settled in very well, getting a place of their own after staying with us for a while. In 1960, we had another house built in Burnaby, where I still live today.

⸺ ● ⸺

In the estimation of most Canadians almost any
dessert is improved with a topping of whipped cream
and it will be a happy day for a lot of people when
they can once more get whipping cream.
– CANADIAN COOK BOOK FOR BRITISH BRIDES

⸺ ● ⸺

Meal time for the younger passengers, with Red Cross
workers feeding the children of seasick mothers.

PHYLLIS PICKFORD

My new life began when I sailed as a twenty-six-year-old war bride with Sandra, my three-year-old daughter, and six-month-old Roger. On November 12, 1946, we left from Liverpool aboard the *Samaria*, a troopship carrying servicemen home.

I last saw my Nana the day I left. She was crying at the garden gate in Beckenham, Kent. She gave me a silver St. Christopher mirror as a parting gift, and I still use it today. My mother escorted us to the train station in London. In tears, she gave me these words to survive by: "If you are ever lonely, look up at the moon and know that we are looking at it too." She also encouraged me to try to be content, even if I had to live in an attic. Strangely enough, I *was* to live in an attic that first winter.

My luggage had gone before me – an old tin trunk and a wooden chest holding old pictures and two family bibles. I carried a case of milk powder, and terry towel diapers. There was no time for emotions on my part. I was busy with a baby-in-arms and a toddler on a harness. I had a husband waiting for me, and my hopes were that the children would have a better life in Canada.

It was a long, rough voyage. We were six days at sea and I was seasick the entire time. Eventually I sent for a doctor who gave me some pills to settle my stomach so I could go to the dining room for a meal. However, as soon as I smelled the food, I rushed to the ship's rail and fed the fish.

I wished that I would die. It was a good thing my mother had given me a little enamel potty, as I had it under my nose throughout the voyage. While I was so sick, a kind lady looked after Sandra and took her to the dining room for her meals.

Our sleeping quarters were a cabin shared with fifteen other women and their babies. We slept in bunks. Sandra shared mine, and Roger was in a rope swing-cot attached to my bunk. Time was spent making up baby formula and washing diapers that we hung from the ship's hot water pipes in our cabins.

I remember one woman who was escorting a child to Canada. The child's mother had been killed in an air raid. I also recall a woman who was very ill after giving birth. Her husband, a serviceman, was in another part of the ship, and, although men were not allowed in our quarters, I gave up my bed for him so he could be near her. One night there was a terrible storm and water rushed in through the porthole. He stuffed it with blankets.

We arrived at Pier 21 on November 18, 1946. I can remember the ship sliding up to dock. I looked up and down at the decks and saw hundreds of women and their children, all searching for someone they knew on shore. There were no immigration or health checks, as this had already been done in England. My husband was waiting for us. I could see him on the dock. One girl asked me, "Is that him? He does look old." I had to agree with her. He had come to meet us in civilian clothing, and the war had taken its toll on him, too. The first night, we slept on the floor at the YMCA. I remember it felt as if the floor was still going up and down.

*Alex McLaughlin
totes flowers,
teddy bear,
and doll as
he meets
his family,
1946.*

At the Halifax railway station, I had my first fried-egg sandwich. It was a real treat, as it was on white bread, which was unattainable in England during the war years. The next day, we took the overnight train to Montreal. The porter carried baby Roger in his arms and rocked him through the night, as he would not settle down. Roger must have missed the motion of his swinging cot on the boat.

We changed trains in Montreal for the journey to Sherbrooke. I thought the trip would never end. We eventually arrived in Lennoxville, where we had to wait for a taxi to take us to a farm. There, we spent our first winter in a two-room attic with no running water, electricity, or indoor toilet. We had to pump water and carry it upstairs in a bucket. There was no sink, just an enamel bowl to use to do the dishes and wash ourselves. We had a pail to empty the water into. The pail was also used as our toilet. When the pail was full, it had to be taken down and emptied outside, behind the barn. We used a Coleman lamp, and for cooking we had a wood stove that was later converted to oil.

I was terribly scared of the rats and mice that kept me awake at night. There were many strange noises called "dingbats." I later learned that these loud bangs were nails in the roof lifting because of frost.

The day after I arrived, it snowed, and I did not see any green grass until the following May. That spring of 1947, I looked in the direction of Lennoxville and saw the town flooded. The St. Francis River had burst its banks, and the land around Bishop's University was under water.

We stayed on the farm for about six months. Then we went to Sherbrooke and stayed with one of my husband's army buddies who lived in a veteran's house. His wife had gone to England to visit her parents, and they rented us their house while she was away. I looked after her husband and made his meals. When his wife returned, we had to vacate. We were at a loss, with nowhere to go. Houses and apartments were still scarce.

I'M GETTING DESPERATE

EXECUTIVE (ex-airforce officer) and wife desire furnished or unfurnished accommodations.

IMMEDIATELY

RETURNED serviceman, wife, child (forced to live apart) require 3 unfurnished rooms. Careful, responsible. . . .

URGENT, BELIEVE IT OR NOT

EX-SERVICEMAN and wife require unfurnished accommodation, west end preferred, references.

VERY URGENT

EX-NAVAL officer and wife (now university students) desperately need furnished accommodations. . . .

Want ads, 1946

Across the road lived an ex-army man who was planning to return to England. I went to see him and asked if we could take over the house if we boarded him until he left for England. He agreed, so we moved in, thinking ourselves lucky to have a house with modern conveniences.

My husband found a job at a pulp and paper plant in Lennoxville, making asbestos tank covers. He worked from six in the morning until six at night. I always had a hot dinner ready when he arrived at home. We did not have much money in those days. The average wage for a man in 1947 was fifty dollars a week. It was the same for all the veterans on our street. To supplement their income, the men used to take part-time jobs. My husband dug potatoes and took his pay in potatoes that would last us all the winter. Other men did bartending or janitorial work, or painted houses.

Not only will there be a welcome for you but there will be extra warmth in it because your husband has gained a place of honour in the minds of his fellow Canadians through serving his country in War.
— WELCOME TO WAR BRIDES

DOROTHY POWELL

Just a brief outline of my meeting with my smashing Canuck. I was a member of the WAAF, and I heard from an old school chum that she was to marry a Canadian and could I get leave to attend the wedding?

I obtained leave and returned to Manchester for her wedding. The night before her big day, we went to the train station to meet her fiancé, Russ, and his father, who also served. Well, Russ also brought

a pal named Ron to act as best man if his
brother couldn't make it. His brother
turned up the next day, and Ron spent
the rest of his leave with me. We kept in
touch for the next few years, and when
he returned from Italy, we married, on
July 31, 1945.

I had to wait for my release from the
air force before I could come to Canada.
I arrived on the *Lady Rodney* on May 24, 1946. For the first several
months, people kept asking if I liked Canada. My answer was always
"I'll tell you when I've been here for the four seasons."

Needless to say, I stayed.

If your husband is already in Canada to receive you,
the arrangements he has made for your home will be
investigated to ascertain if they are suitable for you, as far
as housing conditions will permit.

— WELCOME TO WAR BRIDES

SYLVIA POWER

After high school, I went to an art school, where I stayed for two
years. Then I enlisted in the army, where I worked in a drawing
office. I worked with drafts and plans.

My husband, Douglas, was in the Canadian Medical Corps. His
unit was preparing to follow the D-Day invasion. Both Douglas and I
were working at an ordnance depot, he to prepare unit equipment,
I to work drafting.

Douglas and I met outside a country inn that had a bit of a patio. I remember he kept staring at me. He said it was love at first sight. I just wanted to know what he was staring at!

By the time two weeks were up, we were quite close and promised to write to each other. He said he would be back, and he did write, and he did come back nine months later. He had been stationed in Holland, Belgium, and France.

During that first leave, Douglas proposed to me. But I was scared and uncertain if marrying him was a good idea. It didn't take long for me to be won over. My father was absolutely unwilling to give his permission, though, and you couldn't get married without your parents' permission until you were twenty-one years old. He objected because I was Jewish and Douglas was Catholic.

When Douglas was sent back from the continent, he was stationed at Aldershot, and we were able to take a weekend leave together. In the meantime, I had decided that I would become a Catholic and be made a ward of the court. Douglas knew that we ought to be married before he left, or I would have difficulty coming to Canada. The court process involved a panel of judges and an open discussion of the issues. My father had to be there, and it was a frank and hurtful session. After the ruling that I was a ward of the court, my relationship with my father was strained.

My conversion to Catholicism was not a matter of convenience. I had good instruction from a priest who inspired me to move along the road of my Jewish learning into Christianity.

We got permission to be married and were wed right away, on August 22, 1946. It was an odd wedding: two of the girls from my unit stood for us. The ceremony lasted ten minutes. Eleven days later, Douglas headed back to Canada. My father and my husband got along, and because of that I was able to make up with my family. Douglas spoke with my father before he left for Canada, and this helped my father invite me back into the family home.

After the war, if you were married, you were discharged. I was discharged in September of 1946 and left from Southampton on the

Lady Rodney on November 5, 1946. I remember the date very clearly because it was Guy Fawkes' Night, and for the first time since the war began, Britain was celebrating again. There were bonfires everywhere along the coast.

It was hard to leave London. It was in my blood. I didn't have many possessions to bring to Canada because of the rationing and my time in uniform. Our crossing was cold but sunny. I remember I was offered apples from the Annapolis Valley.

Douglas was waiting at Pier 21 for me. It was the first time I'd seen him in civilian clothes, but I noticed his face – pale green with nerves – more than the suit he had on. His father and sister were very welcoming.

We stayed with his parents for five months. I was pregnant and homesick. I was scared to go to the outdoor toilet by myself. My husband had to take me. I felt very "different" settling into Canada. I felt I had enjoyed things that people in a small town had not, and I swallowed my stories of London to avoid being seen as "putting on airs."

I felt lonely. I had been with a crowd of girls in the army for so long. When my husband left the house each day, I had nowhere to go and I was alone. It was a difficult experience. But involvement

Exhaustion and nervous tension are evident on the faces of Mr. and Mrs. B. Gutteridge as their family reunites in Toronto.

with the church and so on provided some socialization for me. Life in a small town cost you privacy, which I did not like, but it also brought a close-knit community.

We had seven children by the time I got back to England – and I got back by winning a trip. I had really won a trip to the West Indies, and I tried for months to change the deal so I could get to England. I wound up losing everything but the airfare, but at least I was able to go home.

ROSE PURDY

In 1943, I volunteered to join the NAAFI. They had canteens throughout England, serving sailors and soldiers a variety of light meals and refreshments. I was stationed in a Canadian army camp in Witley, Surrey. I was eighteen years old, and my family lived in Muswell Hill, North London. I was very sad that I was not in London with my parents, but at the same time I felt I was doing my "bit" for the war effort.

My job in the canteen was to serve refreshments to the Canadian soldiers, and after a while I noticed this handsome soldier was always hanging around more than the others. We finally got friendly, and he introduced himself as Jack Purdy from St. Catharines, Ontario. We started dating, and the manager of the canteen (a very miserable elderly woman named Mrs. Baker) was warning me on a daily basis that dating a Canadian could have drastic results!

Needless to say, I ignored her and took Jack home to London on leave to meet my parents, who, I might add, thought he was wonderful. They dreaded, however, the thought of me coming to Canada.

Jack and I were married on August 11, 1945, in Our Lady of Muswell Catholic Church in North London. It was a lovely wedding, thanks to my mother's sisters. Clothing was rationed, so I couldn't spend my precious clothing coupons on a wedding dress. My aunt was able to borrow a beautiful white gown. Another aunt made three bridesmaid's dresses for my small cousins. It really turned out to be a lovely wedding day.

When the war ended, Jack went back to Canada, in January 1946. In June I was notified to board the *Aquitania* to Canada. It was an extremely difficult day when I said goodbye to my family, but at the same time I was so excited about coming to Canada. I arrived at Pier 21 after a trip with hundreds of other brides.

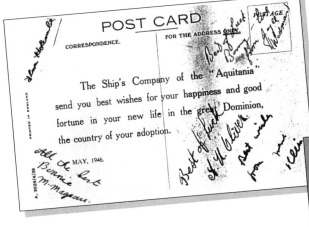

Many brides asked the crew to autograph their souvenir postcards.

Jack was waiting for me in Toronto. It was Dominion Day (now called Canada Day), and I thought I would never survive, because it was very hot. I remember saying to myself, "What on earth have I gotten myself into?" Jack's parents were very good to me and accepted me with open arms.

The first year was the hardest to get accustomed to because of the heat and the snow. We have now been married over fifty-five years. We have one son, one daughter, and two lovely grandchildren. I can honestly say I have no regrets, and I have been fortunate to have married one of the "good" Canadians. I say "good" because I have heard that some war brides weren't quite so lucky.

You are not tied by rationing to deal with any one store
but usually it is a good idea, once you have found a store
you like, to do most of your buying there. You will get better
service and most shopkeepers see that their regular
customers get their fair share of scarce items.
— CANADIAN COOK BOOK FOR BRITISH BRIDES

GRACE SCHWAB

My twenty-one-month-old daughter, Beverley Ann, and I travelled to Canada on the *Britannic* in May 1945. We had two meals a day on board, breakfast and the evening meal. We put our children to bed after they had their evening meal at five and then we had ours at six and seven o'clock. The ship's stewardesses would check the cabins, and if a child was crying, they would try and get them back to sleep. If they couldn't, they called out over the intercom that the mother was wanted, and the mother would leave the table.

Weary war brides and children await the next part of their journey.

The war was still on with Japan. We were in a convoy, and zig-zagged across the ocean because of mines. There was a big American Red Cross ship with wounded on it, and two other ships there to protect us.

Evenings were very quiet. We couldn't go on deck after dark as the ship was blacked out. We sat around in the lounge in the evenings and shed some tears about leaving our families.

After breakfast each day there was a lifeboat drill and we had to put on lifebelts. It was hard to get the little ones into theirs. We had a rough part over the Irish Sea, but when we hit the Gulf Stream it was nice on deck. The food was wonderful on the ship. Someone gave my daughter a banana. She asked me what it was. "It's a banana," I answered. "Do I like them?" she asked. "I don't know," I said, "you'll have to try it." She liked the banana.

We were able to do our washing down in D Deck, where there were lines strung up to hang the clothes on. We had so many things on board that we hadn't seen since the war began that at times I felt guilty, knowing my father and brothers still were receiving little, even my brothers in the forces. A little baby died during our voyage and was buried at sea. We didn't know if it was a boy or a girl. They didn't say. It was so very sad.

Some war brides had their husbands waiting for them in Canada. I think it would have been nice if the government had waited until all the men were back in Canada before sending the wives, but I must say whoever arranged all the passages did a very good job.

When we arrived at Pier 21, a notice was put up telling us how we would disembark – the military first, Air Force, Navy, and then the Army. Then the wives and children of Air Force, Navy and Army in turn. There were Army personnel to help us with luggage and lead us through Pier 21 and onto the trains. We were told that when we married we were Canadian citizens, as were our children.

I rode on the Canadian National Railway to Winnipeg. Along the way we stopped in Quebec and I thought I would buy a newspaper. I didn't realize until I got back on the train that the paper was all in French.

The approximate travelling times from ports of landing to main centres of population in the various Provinces are given hereunder as a guide:—

DESTINATION	FROM HALIFAX	FROM MONTREAL
Montreal, P.Q.	26 hrs.	—
Ottawa, Ont.	29 hrs.	3 hrs.
Toronto, Ont.	33 hrs.	7 hrs.
London, Ont.	36 hrs.	10 hrs.
Windsor, Ont.	40 hrs.	14 hrs.
Port Arthur, Ont.	54 hrs.	28 hrs.
Winnipeg, Man.	62 hrs.	36 hrs.
Regina, Sask.	70 hrs.	44 hrs.
Saskatoon, Sask.	73 hrs.	47 hrs.
Calgary, Alta.	86 hrs.	60 hrs.
Edmonton, Alta.	86 hrs.	60 hrs.
Vancouver, B.C.	114 hrs.	88 hrs.
Victoria, B.C.	120 hrs.	94 hrs.

It should be remembered that these approximate times are based on fast, main line trains. Several hours may have to be added to cover waiting time for connections if the journey is made partly by special and partly by regular trains; also, your new home may be approximately the same distance from the port of landing but located on a branch line where service is slower and less frequent.

Many women had to add ferry and automobile trips to the already lengthy time on the train. From "Welcome to War Brides."

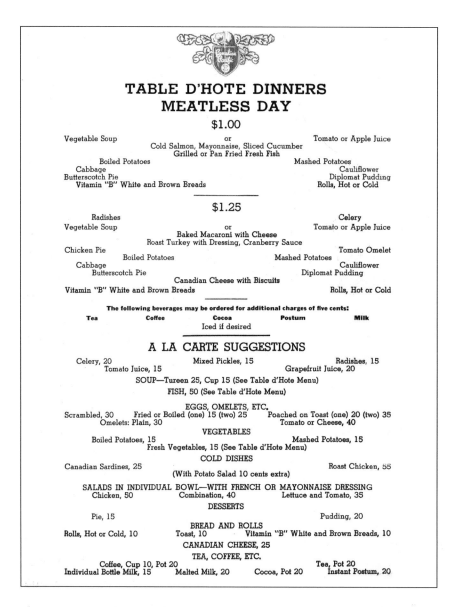

TABLE D'HOTE DINNERS
MEATLESS DAY

$1.00

Vegetable Soup   or   Tomato or Apple Juice

Cold Salmon, Mayonnaise, Sliced Cucumber
Grilled or Pan Fried Fresh Fish

Boiled Potatoes   Mashed Potatoes
Cabbage   Cauliflower
Butterscotch Pie   Diplomat Pudding
Vitamin "B" White and Brown Breads   Rolls, Hot or Cold

$1.25

Radishes   Celery
Vegetable Soup   or   Tomato or Apple Juice

Baked Macaroni with Cheese
Roast Turkey with Dressing, Cranberry Sauce

Chicken Pie   Tomato Omelet
Boiled Potatoes   Mashed Potatoes
Cabbage   Cauliflower
Butterscotch Pie   Diplomat Pudding
Canadian Cheese with Biscuits
Vitamin "B" White and Brown Breads   Rolls, Hot or Cold

The following beverages may be ordered for additional charges of five cents:

Tea   Coffee   Cocoa   Postum   Milk
Iced if desired

A LA CARTE SUGGESTIONS

Celery, 20   Mixed Pickles, 15   Radishes, 15
Tomato Juice, 15   Grapefruit Juice, 20

SOUP—Tureen 25, Cup 15 (See Table d'Hote Menu)

FISH, 50 (See Table d'Hote Menu)

EGGS, OMELETS, ETC.
Scrambled, 30   Fried or Boiled (one) 15 (two) 25   Poached on Toast (one) 20 (two) 35
Omelets: Plain, 30   Tomato or Cheese, 40

VEGETABLES
Boiled Potatoes, 15   Mashed Potatoes, 15
Fresh Vegetables, 15 (See Table d'Hote Menu)

COLD DISHES
Canadian Sardines, 25   Roast Chicken, 55
(With Potato Salad 10 cents extra)

SALADS IN INDIVIDUAL BOWL—WITH FRENCH OR MAYONNAISE DRESSING
Chicken, 50   Combination, 40   Lettuce and Tomato, 35

DESSERTS
Pie, 15   Pudding, 20

BREAD AND ROLLS
Rolls, Hot or Cold, 10   Toast, 10   Vitamin "B" White and Brown Breads, 10

CANADIAN CHEESE, 25

TEA, COFFEE, ETC.
Coffee, Cup 10, Pot 20   Tea, Pot 20
Individual Bottle Milk, 15   Malted Milk, 20   Cocoa, Pot 20   Instant Postum, 20

In those days there was no air conditioning on the train. If one opened the window, all the smoke came in. The meals were wonderful. We ate with the officers; the tables were all set perfectly. I felt sorry for the other ranks, but guess they were just so happy to be going home they didn't care where they ate or slept. I was assigned two bunks, upper and lower, but I couldn't put my little girl in one by herself, so we both slept in one bunk.

When we arrived in Winnipeg, we changed to a Canadian Pacific Railway train. There wasn't much to see, just miles and miles of flat, barren land, and I thought to myself, "What kind of country have I come to?" I was used to passing little villages and seeing houses when riding on trains in England. It took us four days and five nights on the trains to reach Medicine Hat, Alberta.

We had been told to send telegrams to our in-laws as to our time of arrival. The Red Cross also sent them one. The train got emptier as the miles went by. Finally, we arrived at Medicine Hat. It must have been about three in the morning. I forgot that the trains were much higher than in England and one is supposed to wait for the porter to bring the steps, so I stepped down, and broke the heel of my shoe.

There was no place open to get a drink. There was another war bride with two children. I didn't know her. A Red Cross lady came along and said we'd be met by our in-laws, and then the other girl's mother-in-law came along and off they went. My daughter had fallen asleep again, and we sat there and sat there. One of the workmen came along and offered to fix the heel on my shoe, which he did, and then left. We still waited. Many years later, I thought I should have gone to a hotel, but in those days young ladies didn't do things like that. I had led a rather sheltered life. I think if someone had come along and said, "Would you like to go back to England?" then I would have jumped at the offer!

It got to be seven o'clock, and we were cold and tired. A porter must have gotten in touch with the Red Cross, for a woman came up to me and said, "Are you still here?" She said the mayor had been told of my arrival, and he had gone and told my mother-in-law what time the train was coming in. She said they had also received two telegrams. It was now 7:30, and the Red Cross lady said she would take me to them. I gave her the address, and when we arrived at the house, she knocked on the door, and my mother-in-law said she didn't know I was coming.

I had expected a warm welcome, which I certainly did not get. I stayed for two weeks. My brother-in-law and his wife came to see me

FARMS OR ACREAGE WANTED

THE DIRECTOR, The Veterans' Land Act, is interested in obtaining particulars of farms varying in size from 40-100 acres or more, carrying productive soil and equipped with habitable buildings and satisfactory water supply, favourably located in regard to markets, schools and social services; also acreage suitably located for small holdings, either with or without buildings, adjacent to or adjoining cities, towns or villages in Ontario, where there are reasonable prospects for employment in industry, commerce or agriculture.

LANDS of the above type are required for the re-establishment of veterans of the Canadian Active Service Forces and the Director is prepared to purchase outright for cash such lands as are found suitable for this purpose.

FOR the guidance of all owners of land who may be interested in this advertisement the following quotation from The Veterans' Land Act, 1942, is important:—

> "No person, firm or corporation shall be entitled to charge or to collect as against or from any other person, firm or corporation any fee or commission or advance of price for services rendered in the sale of any land made to the Director, whether for the finding or introducing of a buyer or otherwise."

Address all replies to

C. M. NIXON, District Superintendent, The Veterans' Land Act, 21 Lombard Street, Toronto

The Veterans' Land Act provided for low-cost loans to those who wanted to purchase property after the war. The Act also helped the men buy other materials, like farm machinery and livestock.

and said if they had known they would have met us. They had been told not to bother, as my mother-in-law was going to meet us. I had never felt so alone. After two weeks I couldn't stand it any longer. I went and stayed a week with my sister-in-law. She was friendlier, but she had five children, so room was very scarce.

I walked to the rental office. They didn't have anything available, and returning veterans had priority. The man must have felt sorry for me, as he told me to call the next day and see him. The next day, I went to see him, and he said he still didn't have anything, but he had talked to his wife and she agreed I could rent their basement. It was one large room with a little kitchen area, which did fine. The rent was affordable. I had sent my daughter's crib with the other baggage, so she had a bed to sleep in. The couple was very kind to me.

I went to the bank to see if my money from England had been transferred. The bank manager informed me that my mother-in-law had been in with the cheque and tried to cash it. He had tried to explain to her that, as it wasn't hers, he would keep it, and that she should tell me he would like to see me. I never got the message. When I did go to see him, he said he had also found my army dependent cheque, which my mother-in-law had tried to cash.

I spent a very lonely six months before my husband, Philip, returned in December 1945. No one came to check on how I was doing. It was my little girl who kept me going. When either one of us were ill, there were no arrangements made for it. I found it hard finding the money for a doctor and medications.

I never wrote and told my dad and brothers. It would have worried them. When I knew my husband was actually on his way, I got a flat and some furniture, so when he came everything was in place. I remember being told that things were rationed, but my goodness, compared to the rationing I was used to, things here were plentiful.

Philip arrived home in December 1945, six months after Beverley Ann and I came to Canada. On his first night home, we went to tuck our daughter into bed. I asked Beverley Ann if she was going to kiss her daddy goodnight. "I've got to kiss my little daddy first," she said, and she kissed the small photograph of her father that we kept next to her bed. Then she kissed Philip, and she wouldn't let him out of her sight after that.

The first couple of years were hard, as all the jobs had been taken up by the men who had already returned, but our love was strong. Twenty-three years passed before I was able to visit England for the first time. Sadly, our daughter who came with me died in October 1987. Otherwise, life has been good to us.

You will become intimately acquainted with tomatoes,
while some old friends like Brussels sprouts, winter greens
and broad beans, you will meet only occasionally.
— CANADIAN COOK BOOK FOR BRITISH BRIDES

JOAN SMALE

I well remember my voyage across the Atlantic on the *Aquitania* in June 1946. I didn't find it a particularly rough crossing, but many girls suffered from bouts of seasickness. Several times, I was the only person at my table in the dining room.

What a thrill it was to enter Halifax Harbour, although the dock area didn't really impress me. We disembarked according to eventual destination, and those for Toronto were among the last to leave. After two days and nights on the train, I began to realize what a vast country I had chosen to be my future home.

On July 1, I was greeted by my husband and in-laws at Toronto's Union Station. Unfortunately, I became a deserted wife when my Canadian-born son was a year old. Nevertheless, I have absolutely no regrets about becoming a true Canadian. One of these days I hope to be able to visit Halifax again and see Pier 21 in its new role.

JEAN SPEAR

I was in London just after war was declared. At sixteen, I was about to have my first holiday alone. My father was with me, and when the sirens announced an air raid, the police directed us to basements.

We ended up in the basement of the Patent Office, where we waited, standing shoulder to shoulder amongst dusty documents until the all-clear sounded. We had expected to come up to a destroyed London, but we found that the sun was shining and nothing had happened.

After I finished high school, I decided I wanted a career in journalism and eventually was offered a job at *Woman* magazine. Each day, I travelled to London and worked for the woman who wrote the "answers to the lovelorn" letters. I typed the answers and got them ready for printing. My boss had a fondness for martinis and would have two at lunch. Afternoons were completely unproductive, and so I began to draft the answers. Before I knew it, I was writing all the answers to the letters, and I was still only sixteen.

My job at the magazine stopped one day when I arrived at work and found a huge hole where the office building had been. After the shock began to wear off, I went home, and my father would never let me go back into London to work again. I took a local job in an electrical insulation factory, where I looked after orders and dispatches.

During the war, the English girls' one love that we were still able to do was dancing. It was very important to us. Girls tried not to go to these dances in pairs, because we wanted to be alone in case someone interesting came along. I met my husband, George, in 1941, at a dance studio called the Palais de Danse. I was wearing a red silk dress when George asked me to dance. We danced all night and then he walked me home.

The next day we went swimming, and then back to our house for tea. While we were having tea, my mother invited George to come and visit us when he next had leave. (This gives you a little indication of the trust and welcome there was at that time.)

George came and spent the next week with us. We were a twosome from that time onwards. George was a sergeant. Then, at the age of twenty-one, he became a sergeant major. The local British companies would not believe that someone so young could have his rank. But George was a very good soldier, and he enjoyed being in the army.

One day, George and I decided to rent a boat. (We lived near the Thames.) The proprietor agreed to rent a canoe to George because he was a Canadian soldier. We also went skating – George played on a Canadian hockey team in London. He became a part of the family.

There was a wide variety of men in England during the war: South Africans, Australians, Poles, and Americans. I used to say that all the Englishmen were gone. I lost several former boyfriends during the war.

My younger sister met an American, and we often double-dated. She eventually married the man and moved to Kentucky. She had known him for only three months and then he was sent back to the United States to get his wings. He never returned, but three years later he sent for her and she sailed to New York to meet him.

During our courtship, George was often away on courses in Italy and Wales. I never knew, when I said goodbye, where he was going. I always waited for the first phone call that said he'd gotten back safely. The uncertainty was the hardest thing to bear; you just held your breath. The mail was the most important link. Everything continued, but in some ways my life was on hold while I waited to hear from George.

George and I were an item for about a year before we married. I think it was remarkable that we waited for so long. Although I was only nineteen when we married, I didn't feel young. I felt mature and very sure of myself. Nobody raised any objections, and I had been in touch with George's family. My future in-laws sent me lingerie for my wedding, because clothes in England were rationed. My mother-in-law also sent a three-tiered wedding cake, in separate packages. The third tier arrived just in time, but the sugar for the icing didn't make it. I don't know how we found enough sugar to make icing, but we did.

My wedding dress was a white form-fitting princess-line style made in satin. I had a long veil and a bouquet. The gown was borrowed from the local butcher's daughter, who had gotten married the week before we did. I had to return it to the woman after our wedding.

Jean and George Spear (Lieutenant in the Royal Canadian Engineers) shortly after their marriage.

We were married on August 22, 1942, at Norburton Church, where my grandfather was the warden. He passed the collection plate around because the church was so full. Normally, this was not done, and I didn't know about it until later. We had a guard of honour, and George had drilled the men, telling them that they could not be out drinking beforehand or else he would lay charges.

We honeymooned on the west coast seashore. A friend of mine loaned George some civilian clothes, so I saw him in "normal" clothes for the first time on our honeymoon. The clothes made him a very different-looking man. I'm glad I didn't have the shock of heading for Canada and not liking what my husband looked like out of uniform.

One day in 1944, when George was supposed to be in Italy, I heard footsteps on the stairs and it was him. He had had a call to return to Canada to set up an intelligence course on the west coast. He made arrangements with the Red Cross for me to travel to Canada. Because of the work he was doing with Intelligence, George knew that the V-2 rockets were coming, and he wanted me out of there.

In December 1944, I got a call to take the train to Waterloo Station. My mum and dad knew I was leaving, but none of the other relatives did. I had to say goodbye, but they didn't know it really was "goodbye." My dad travelled to Waterloo with me. As I walked towards the exit, he walked about six paces behind me. A lady in a Red Cross uniform introduced herself and asked who I was. She told me to follow her, and I didn't say goodbye to my dad. I turned and waved to him, not knowing if I would ever see him again. I didn't.

The Red Cross lady and I took a taxi to a townhouse in London that was full of war brides and little kids. Later, there was a long, tiring trip to Liverpool. I climbed aboard the *Louis Pasteur*, and when I went down to my cabin I found there were sixteen other bunks in it and I was on a top bunk. It was a rough crossing.

When we arrived in Halifax, everyone was told to gather in a lounge on board. I asked for something to drink and was given a Coca-Cola. I had never tasted one before. It was full of ice cubes, and I'd never had them before either. It was the most delicious drink I have ever had!

As I stood there, a young sailor came towards me. It was Buddy, my brother-in-law. He had somehow found out what ship I was on and got permission to board it. This was remarkable – I had a welcome to Canada that not everybody had. I fell in love with Canada as soon as I stepped onto firm ground. My parents-in-law always told me that I was the best Canadian that they had ever met.

I boarded a train for a trip that I thought was absolutely wonderful. I arrived in Ottawa on December 23 at about eleven o'clock at night. When the train stopped, I got off, but didn't realize that I was supposed to walk through the train to get to the place where the platform started. I was up to my knees in snow! As I began to walk toward the main part of the station, a young man in uniform rushed toward me. It was George. I had no idea he would be there at the station. He might have been back in Italy, or on the West Coast of Canada. It was the happiest moment of my life. I had Christmas that year with my in-laws, and it was the first time in five years that George's parents had both of their sons home for the holiday.

I don't think I was prepared for what Canada was like. All we had for information and background were the stories that our husbands told us. Some of the stories were greatly embellished, but those I heard were accurate and down-to-earth. During my first winter in Canada, I saw the clear blue sky and the snow and I thought I had never seen anything so lovely. I enjoyed the winters, and then summer came along and it was hot!

For a time, George was posted to British Columbia. Later he was sent to Debert, Nova Scotia, where he was demobbed. We had a cottage on the seashore. Then George joined the public service in Ottawa.

In 1945, the Red Cross decided to establish a club for the war brides who were arriving from England. The club met in the YWCA building in Ottawa. Initially, the Red Cross helped organize things, but soon afterwards the war brides did it on their own. The club was named the ESWIC (England, Scotland, Wales, Ireland, Canada) Club.

The club turned out to be a lifeline for the war brides. It provided social occasions when they could meet and talk about home and how it compared to Canada. We tried very hard to become good Canadians. We had speakers from the departments of agriculture and health. We spoke with reporters and politicians and tried to broaden our knowledge of Canada. We had a lot of fun at the same time.

We had our own welfare program where we looked after any war bride who was having difficulties, and we contacted all the social welfare offices to collect the right information to pass along. The club sent parcels back to England, including food packages for families the club "adopted" in London. We also used to collect magazines that we delivered to hospitals, supported various charities, and raised funds by having bazaars.

The club also organized dances and parties, and this is where the association with Lady Clutterbuck, the British High Commissioner's wife, began. She attended the bazaars and invited the club members to the official residence, Earnscliffe, where the club held its garden parties. Lady Clutterbuck was a marvellous woman, and the association with Earnscliffe has continued through the years. We had our club's fiftieth reunion there in 1995. We also had a fifty-fifth reunion

Top: *Jean Spear pins a corsage on Lady Clutterbuck
as ESWIC members look on, 1952.
Bottom: Earnscliffe, once the home of Sir John A. Macdonald.*

in the summer of 2000, because we wanted to have one in the new millennium. We had tea at Earnscliffe and the next day went to Rideau Hall, where we received a signed picture of Governor General Adrienne Clarkson. I have taken care of the club memorabilia since the beginning.

I have no recollection of anything but the feeling that I was at home when I landed in Halifax. Canada is where I belong.

Note of Appreciation

By Lt. Col. W.E. Sutherland OBE
Ship's Commandant
17 Sept. 46

TO ALL CANADIAN WIVES ON BOARD H.M.T. "QUEEN MARY"

Each Voyage as we approach our destination I always like
to say a few words to the Troops and Wives of Service personnel on board and this time not only can I commend most
highly their pleasant co-operation but I warmly thank all
on board for the manner in which you have fallen in with
Trooping routine.

This is the last Voyage of the "Queen Mary" as a
Troopship. You 1700 Service Dependents and over 600
Ministry of War Transport Civilians alike, must feel just
a little proud in making the final Voyage on a Ship that
has such a marvellous war record in the transportation of
hundreds of thousands of Troops to the battle fronts of
the world.

Many of your husbands went over to Britain on this
same Ship as she zig zagged through the then dangerous
waters, unguarded and alone, eluding the submarines that
vainly tried so often to intercept her.

Canada is just ahead. To most of you it ushers in the
advent of a new life with new adventures and responsibili-
ties, the success or failure of which depends on the
stability and determination of each individual. I am
absolutely confident that you will not only be worthy
of the confidence and trust imposed in you by Canada's
fighting men, but that you will be citizens that Canada
may justly be proud of.

There awaits you in the sheltered harbour of Halifax a
welcome the warmth of which will extend from one end of
the Dominion to the other. Canada welcomes you with a deep
feeling of pride -- you who are truly representative of the
remarkable womanhood of Britain, who during the long dark
years of war, stood up so courageously, who sacrificed so
bravely, and who contributed so materially to the magnifi-
cent war effort -- all of which won the deep admiration of
all the decent peoples of the world.

British stock such as this is indeed a welcome addition
to our country; and your lovely children, the likes of
which I have never seen surpassed, should grow up under

Canada's sunny skies, true stalwarts of parents who have proven their worth as real men and women -- and on their shoulders will rest the future responsibility of guiding the National Affairs of State and the future destiny of Canada.

Going through the Nurseries on the Ship and looking into the faces of these lovely children, I so often think of the quotation read by Prime Minister Mackenzie King, in giving his fine talk to all on board last Voyage when he read -- Quote "The tiniest bits of opinion sown in the minds of children in private life afterwards issue forth to the world and become a public opinion; for Nations are gathered out of Nurseries, and they who hold the leading strings of children may even exercise a greater power than those who hold the reins of Government." End of Quote.

You have had on this Voyage another message of welcome from one of Canada's great men in public life — The Hon. Mr. Ilsley, Minister of Finance in the Government of Canada. I hope and feel that you will always remember the message given you by the Hon. Mr. Ilsley and may it be a source of inspiration to you in the days ahead.

Canada is indeed a vast country. Her nine great Provinces stretch over an expanse of varied land 3000 miles in extent, from Halifax to Vancouver. You will be impressed by the tremendous development achieved and also by the great natural resources yet to be developed. You should also be proud to remember that in Canada's early settlement it was many of your pioneering forebearers from England, Scotland and Ireland who by great industry and unsurpassed fortitude hewed out their homesteads and built the foundation for a great Canada. Preserve well this heritage handed down to you through generations.

To all of you GOOD BYE — GOOD LUCK — AND GOD BLESS YOU.

                          [signed] W. E. Sutherland
                          (W.E. Sutherland) Lt-Col.
                               Ship's Commandant
                               H.M.T. "Queen Mary"

[A note on Sutherland's copies of his farewell letters notes that the *Aquitania* was used after the *Queen Mary* left the trooping service. Sutherland was the Ship's Commandant of the *Aquitania* at the end of her "glorious record of trooping," and wrote a "good luck" letter to the brides aboard on February 6, 1947, the ship's last such voyage. The *Aquitania* was replaced by the *Samaria*.]

You know, of course, how fond your husband is of "pie."
In that he is like almost every other Canadian.
— CANADIAN COOK BOOK FOR BRITISH BRIDES

JOHANNA (JOAN) TAYLOR

I met my husband, Raymond, while he was serving in the Royal Navy on a trawler that was converted into a minesweeper called the *Powis Castle*. The ship's main home port was Stornoway, Isle of Lewis. Next to the quay where the ship docked was an establishment called Mac's Imperial Bar, and it was a favourite watering hole for any sailor back from a tour.

Mac's also featured a tea room on the upper level. My friend Violet and I served tea there. Violet had a friend named Shem, who was a Newfoundlander serving overseas as a Forester. Shem, in turn, was a friend of Ray's. The relationship between Violet and Shem (they later married) led to the meeting of Ray and me.

I lived on a croft with my family, in a small village called Balallan, outside of Stornoway. The wind there can be quite strong, and on the night Ray proposed to me, the wind blew his bonnet clean from his head the moment he asked me to marry him. He lost his bonnet, but he won me.

My journey to Canada began on a day in March 1946. A message came that said I was to leave from Liverpool on the *Scythia*. Until the message arrived, I had given very little thought as to when this would happen, although deep down in my heart, I knew the day would eventually come. I would have to leave our beloved Isle of Lewis.

I had two sons, one three years old, the other three months old, and the very thought of travelling across the Atlantic Ocean was rather frightening to say the least. Ray had been discharged. The

cruel six-year war was finally over, but not without taking its toll of young men, among them two of my brothers.

The stark reality of having to leave my parents, brothers, and sisters, was indeed heartbreaking. There were moments when I wondered if I could face up to it. There were hundreds of others leaving, but knowing they were feeling the same way gave little comfort to me at the time. Also, my mother tongue was Gaelic, not English, so I knew I would have some difficulty settling in Canada.

We three left Stornoway in a small plane that took us to Glasgow. From there, we travelled by train to Liverpool, en route to Halifax on the *Scythia*, and then on to St. John's, Newfoundland on the *Baccalieu*.

I shall never forget everyone's tears and goodbyes. We had to line up to board buses that took us to dockside. At one point, my arms ached as I held a child in each arm. I had a small suitcase with some necessities, and while still waiting in the line, I laid down my suitcase and sat on it. My three-year-old sat on the ground by me. I could easily have burst into tears right then, but didn't, simply because it would have upset the children. I thought to turn back home.

The pipe band played "Auld Lang Syne" as our ship sailed away from the pier and then I surely gave way to the tears I could no longer hold back.

It was a good crossing, although the weird sounds of foghorns and the creaking of the ship added to our feelings of loneliness. Once or twice I went to the promenade deck. All that was to be seen was the broad Atlantic Ocean, so I decided to stay close to my quarters with my two little ones. I felt safe there.

We were very fortunate not to be seasick and we enjoyed to the fullest the elaborate meals prepared for us. When we arrived in Halifax, we were transferred to the *Baccalieu*. It was a rough crossing to Newfoundland. The crew said it was the worst they had experienced in fifteen years. At one point, I got to my feet unsteadily, held on to whatever I could grasp, and began making my way to the bathroom. A sack of sugar burst through a cupboard door and I was knocked down. One of the crew came to my rescue, helped me to the bathroom, and then led me back to my cabin.

Nearly everyone was so sick they couldn't move. I think I was too numb with fear, and caring for my children, so I wasn't ill. The decks were awash, and whenever the program "Decks Awash" was shown on television I thought of my voyage from Halifax to St. John's. After all this time it is still quite vivid in my mind.

When we arrived in St. John's, Ray and his parents were anxiously waiting, as they were aware that our crossing had been a stormy one. I must have been in a sort of daze while I prepared to get off the boat. After getting the children dressed, I sat on the edge of my bunk, unable to move and holding my children close to me. Everyone was streaming out through the corridors, but there I sat, making no effort to leave the boat.

Then I heard my husband asking one of the crew where my cabin was, and I called out "Here I am!" and we clung together. There were

Dad tentatively peeks into the basket as his wife, Rea Conroy, chats with her in-laws at the train station.

more tears, but at last I felt safe and secure. I walked off the boat with him, and when I met his family I knew I belonged. They were such warm people.

ANNA THOMPSON

The journey on the *Queen Mary* in 1946 was fine for me, but one day out it got rough, and the lady in my quarters had a set of twin babies. She got very ill and I was able to help with the twins – quite a novelty for me.

When we arrived in Halifax, we were a long time getting off the ship, and when I did and found my luggage, I couldn't find my husband, Lorimer. He had waited so long he had decided to look for refreshments. So he wasn't there when we finally disembarked. He wasn't missing for long, though. For supper, I was taken to a restaurant, and my husband ordered my meal. I found a large ear of corn at the edge of my plate. "But that's chicken feed!" I said. "What do I do with that?" During his demonstration, hubby got to eat both ears!

Also, with his being in civilian clothes, and with a one-and-a-half year absence, Lorimer didn't look like the man I married!

Never mind, nine months later I delivered a baby girl.

If you can make good doughnuts your husband will think you're wonderful! On the other hand, you can buy them.
— CANADIAN COOK BOOK FOR BRITISH BRIDES

RUBY THORNE

I left England on board the *Britannic* and arrived in Halifax in May 1945. Two days later, I arrived in Saint John, New Brunswick, and lived with my husband Ken's sister.

Ken came back from Germany in June 1945. We lived with his sister for three months because we couldn't get an apartment. We couldn't get an apartment because we had a child – if you had a dog you could get an apartment, but not if you had a child.

We found one room and lived in it for nine months, and then we got an apartment. I didn't think much of Canada then.

Ken rejoined the forces in 1947 and things were much better. We had postings in Ontario, New Brunswick, and Germany. When Ken retired from the forces I thought "Civvy Street" was for the birds, but I got used to it after two years.

We came to Vancouver in 1971. I joined the local war bride's club in 1996. All told, life in Canada has been good.

KAY WAGNER

During the war, I was in the National Fire Service, stationed at Lewes, Sussex. David, my husband-to-be, was with the Third Division, Royal Canadian Corps of Signals. We married on July 1, 1943.

As I think back, the move to Canada certainly was an undertaking for us. I guess we were young and adventurous, and *in love*. I sailed on the *Scythia* in February 1946. We were twenty-four hours out when we encountered heavy seas and an engine went out. We started to list very badly and it was a major feat to stand up. My parents heard the SOS call on their radio before we were aware of it ourselves on board. It was announced we were returning to port, and we figured it would be Liverpool. But tugs towed us into Belfast Lough. One of our brides had developed pregnancy problems and she was lowered over the side and taken to Belfast City Hospital.

We set sail again with a renewed supply of milk and fresh water. The journey was quite pleasant after that.

The exciting part was when they announced we should soon see land. I took my nineteen-month-old daughter up on deck with me and finally saw the shoreline. I had never seen frozen sea before, and an ice-breaker was ahead of us. It seemed forever until we came up to the dock.

I will always remember a little white church set up on a hill, just like a picture postcard. We hugged the rails so we wouldn't miss the new sights. The band played for us and we watched as the girls disembarked for the east. The "west" brides would get off the next day.

Aerial View of the Business Section, Halifax, Nova Scotia.   R.C.A.F. Picture. 11.

Everything looked so grey and dull. I watched the crane lifting the luggage out of the hold and swinging it over to where it was placed in the sheds. We joked and said that if our trunks contained china, it was in a million pieces by now.

I spent a restless night in anticipation of what the next day would bring. We were called to Customs by our surname. I have always wondered who was so smart in making up the questions. The one I have never forgotten was "Do you plan on staying in Canada?" At that point, I hadn't even set foot on Canadian soil!

I guess my answer was good enough, as two soldiers came to help me leave the ship, carrying my suitcases and daughter. We went into the shed and walked along past signs for each letter of the alphabet until we found the "Ws." I realized then it had been a good idea to paint a big white "W" on my trunks. After identifying them, we proceeded to the train. It was cold and wet, just plain gloomy.

The fellows found my seat, put my suitcases in place, and wished me the best of luck. It was just minutes until a representative of the Anglican Church came with a cup of tea and biscuits. I had left home on February 17. Now it was March 1, and I was on the train in Canada. I can hardly believe we made the trip, with washing, meals, trying to sleep, and, most of all, wondering what it was going to be like and whether the man in my life was going to be there at the end of the journey.

He was – and we have raised six children. I have never been sorry I came to Canada.

We certainly shan't try to tell you how to make a good cup of tea but you might find some pointers on coffee making useful.
— CANADIAN COOK BOOK FOR BRITISH BRIDES

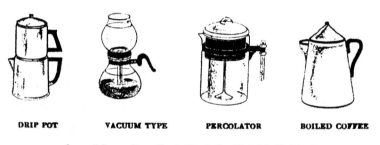

| DRIP POT | VACUUM TYPE | PERCOLATOR | BOILED COFFEE |

from "Canadian Cook Book for British Brides"

ROSALIND WALSH

The *Île de France* sailed from Southampton on April 2, 1946. On board were five thousand Canadian servicemen and thirty war brides and husbands. It had been an emotional farewell at the dockside for the young women. Canada was a long way from family and friends, six days by ocean liner.

The wives had separate quarters on board ship. They joined their husbands for breakfast. We passed the time strolling the decks and chatting during the long voyage. The ship was overcrowded – troops

Rosalind
and
Louis
Walsh

slept in hammocks below deck. It was wall-to-wall soldiers. They were uncomfortable, but happy to be homeward bound at last.

For those who were ill, it was not a pleasure cruise. Meals were served twice daily. There was a terrific menu, and the food was displayed on elegant tables, with white tablecloths, no less. It was a pleasant surprise to many of us that we could purchase whole cartons of chocolate bars in the ship's canteen.

Fire drill was our only activity. No quoits or shuffleboard on board for entertainment. Reading, playing cards, and holding long conversations about our plans for the future seemed to be the only pastimes. Our lives had been focused on war; peacetime was an unknown factor to many of us. A number of the returning soldiers talked of broken marriages or hasty weddings before their departure overseas. Others spoke of sweethearts left behind, and friends who would not be returning home.

As the *Île de France* sailed into Halifax, everyone went out on deck to catch a glimpse of the Canadian shoreline. It looked welcoming, but foreign. Halifax in those days was drab and grey. The wooden houses resembled apple crates turned upside down. Some passengers

Barrington Street, Halifax, Nova Scotia. —65.

went ashore but most stayed on board. Several came back to report that the clothing stores had outdated styles and "old-lady shoes."

Bright and early the next morning, the troops were marched to their trains, some bound for the Canadian West, others for Ontario and Nova Scotia and Newfoundland. The trains were huge compared to our small British ones. The whistles had such a melancholy wail.

The volunteers who assisted throughout the land journey (arranging meals, locating baggage, and handling the paperwork) did a commendable job in undertaking the enormous task of welcoming the newcomers to Canada. Upon our arrival in North Sydney, Nova Scotia, we were sent to several hotels to spend the night. It was something of a shock when we were assigned two couples to a room. Of course, this was refused, and we tossed a coin to see which couple would seek other accommodations.

Everyone was delighted to be on terra firma once more. But not for long. The Cabot Straits lay ahead. "The stormiest crossing in years," said the sailors as the vessel heaved its way across the Gulf of St. Lawrence. It was a long, sleepless night for most of us. At six the next morning, everyone rushed on deck to catch sight of the

The Nova Scotian and C.N.R. Station, Halifax, Nova Scotia, Canada.—31.

POST CARD

July 28th/46

Have just spent a week of my
vacation at This Hotel in Halifax.
I saw three liners come in—
the "Queen Mary", the "Lady Nelson"
and the "Aquatania". The "Queen
Mary" brought war-brides to
Canada but the Aquatania brot
a lot of troops as well as war-
brides. It was wonderful to
watch the "Queen Mary" being
brot to the pier by the tiny tugs.
What are you doing now? I
was pleased to get your card.
Don't work too hard. Keep well.
Dorothy.

Miss Betty Ulrici.
38 Park Avenue.
Wakefield.
Mass..
U.S.A.

Newfoundland coastline. There, looming ahead, fogbound and for-
bidding, was the ominous Rock. After we docked in the dense fog at
Port aux Basques, we had difficulty making out the figures of the
longshoremen, wearing their oilskins, logan boots, and sou'westers.
Snow lay everywhere. The ship had sailed from springtime back into
winter. No one spoke. The "Newfie Bullet" awaited. It ran on a
narrow-gauge railway track, three-and-a-half feet wide, and made the

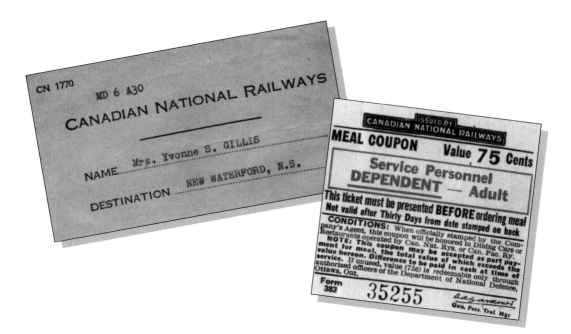

three-hundred-mile trip to St. John's in seventy-two hours. Because it was a social occasion, the crew didn't keep to the schedule.

The stewards were friendly. The menu on board was regional fare: cod tongues, brewis, scruncheons, trout, bakeapple jam, and salt-beef dinner. The scenery was bleak: rocks, barrens, and endless snow-drifts. But inside the train was the real Newfoundlander, at home in his native land, kindly, humorous, and generous. As the train chugged its way across the country, numerous stops were made at quaint-sounding places like Goobies, Come By Chance, and Topsail. When the war brides and their children alighted at their destinations, they looked back at the train as it pulled away. It was a last link with home.

St. John's railway station was a hive of activity, and what an affectionate welcome the veterans received from their families. Most of the men had been overseas for the entire six years of the war. It was an apprehensive moment for their wives, who didn't know how they'd be received, but for most it was a pleasant experience.

The drive along Water Street, which was the main thoroughfare, passed several stores, as they called them, not shops as in Britain.

Bowrings, Ayre and Sons, the Bon Marché, the London New York and Paris. No supermarkets in those days; most of the grocery stores were corner shops. The local fishermen called at your front door weekly, selling codfish and cod roe, twenty-five cents for a full fish. A fresh salmon cost a dollar if you went down to Portugal Cove where the fishermen sold them. We often went down on a Sunday to scoop up basinfuls of caplin when they washed ashore.

The cathedral was the tallest building in the city. Life was pretty rugged back then in Newfoundland; houses seemed to cling to the sides of cliff faces, steep hills everywhere, and many homes with no indoor plumbing. I soon learned what "the midnight patrol" meant. All of the water to my father-in-law's home on Signal Hill was carted uphill in buckets, a primitive lifestyle and a setback for me, coming from a big city in Scotland. I decided to move out as soon as possible, which we did.

During the summer months one could forget the travails of life and enjoy the good times. We fished in the many "ponds," as they called their lakes. We went berry-picking for cranberries, blueberries, and bakeapples. We went down to the sea often to gaze towards the horizon and visualize the coastline of Scotland. In time, we all became involved with the business of raising families, setting up house, and finding jobs. We formed the Rose and Thistle Club, and enjoyed meeting in the afternoons and for other social occasions.

The Newfoundland women were kindness itself, good-hearted and fun-loving. They're terrific bakers; their dark fruitcake, loaded with cherries, raisins, nuts, molasses, and spices, was a treat. Especially when accompanied by a quaff of homemade blueberry wine. Being invited to a "time," which was another name for a party, meant a "scoff," with salt-beef dinner, pease pudding, and steam duff. There was lots of singing, dancing, and music of the homemade variety, a winter's evening activity with the more people the merrier.

My husband, Louis, found a good job; we prospered and had a family. We were transferred to Nova Scotia in 1959 by his company, and again in 1966 to Ontario. At that time, it was for the best, as employment was scarce in St. John's and we knew that one day our children would leave. This way, we went ahead before they did. We spent thirteen years in Newfoundland, and after the move to Ontario we retired to British Columbia.

Perhaps Newfoundlanders no longer boil the kettle and fry freshly caught trout by the side of a "pond" as we did, but then again maybe they do. I bet they no longer use the old sayings, like "bound you will." And the Newfoundlander's toast:

I bows towards you,
I nods accordant . . .
I catches your eye and I smiles.

Acknowledgments

Heartfelt thanks are extended to all the war brides and their families who shared their stories with the staff of the Pier 21 Society Resource Centre and me. Special thanks to Carrie-Ann Smith, Research Librarian, Pier 21, Halifax, for her invaluable aid, often at a moment's notice, during the compilation of this book. My sincere gratitude as well to Mary Tulle, General Manager of Pier 21; to Steven Schwinghamer and Amy Coleman of the Pier 21 Resource Centre; to David Bennett of Transatlantic Literary Agency; to Tom Kneebone; to David Campbell; to friends who shared the names of brides; to John Critchley, who kindly replied to an e-mail from a stranger; and to Cal Smiley, "courier extraordinaire." Finally, a thank-you to Kathy Lowinger for her encouragement; to Jonathan Webb, for taking on a "rookie"; and to my McClelland & Stewart friends, Alex Schultz and Kong Njo, for their guidance and enthusiasm.

Note

There are, of course, thousands of other "war-bride stories" out there. Those interested in sharing their stories are welcome to contribute them to the Pier 21 Resource Centre holdings. Please send them to the Librarian, Pier 21 Society, 1055 Marginal Road, Halifax, Nova Scotia, B3J 4P6, or submit the story electronically via the Pier 21 Society Web site at pier21.ns.ca.

Credits

Grateful acknowledgement is made to all those who have granted permission to reprint copyrighted and personal material. Every reasonable effort has been made to locate the copyright holders for these images. The publishers would be pleased to receive information that would allow them to rectify any omissions in future printings.

Front cover: courtesy of Micki More; *4:* Pier 21 Society; *6:* author's collection; *7:* NFB/National Archives of Canada (hereafter NAC)/C-026989; *8:* City of Toronto Archives (hereafter CTA), SC 266, item 104103; *9:* CTA, SC 266, item 101058; *11:* courtesy of John Critchley, England; *13:* CTA, SC 266, item 102518; *16:* author's collection; *19:* Pier 21 Society; *20:* Pier 21 Society; *23:* Pier 21 Society; *26:* author's collection; *29:* Pier 21 Society, Allan S. Tanner Collection; *33:* Pier 21 Society; *35:* author's collection; *37:* Pier 21 Society; *38 – 40:* courtesy of Ivy M. Feltmate; *41:* Pier 21 Society; *42:* courtesy of Irene Griffin; *43:* used with permission, Communications Nova Scotia on behalf of the Nova Scotia government; *49:* from *Halifax in Wartime*, courtesy of the family of Robert W. Chambers; *52, left:* author's collection; *right:* courtesy of Margaret Chase Huxford; *55:* courtesy of Eileen Ironside; *58:* Pier 21 Society; *60:* author's collection; *64:* Pier 21 Society; *66, top:* CTA, SC 266, item 102523; *bottom:* courtesy of Jeannie (Jenny) MacKinnon; *70:* CTA, SC 266, item 102521; *71:* courtesy of Dorothy McIlveen; *73:* author's collection; *75:* Pier 21 Society; *77:* CTA, SC 266, item 101403; *81:* courtesy of Olive Minnings; *82:* Pier 21 Society; *83 – 84:* courtesy of Micki More; *86:* courtesy of Phyllis Oliver; *87:* Pier 21 Society; *89:* Pier 21 Society; *93:* NAC/PA112368; *inset:* Pier 21 Society; *96:* courtesy of Florence Phillips; *99:* NAC/PA175792; *101:* CTA, SC 266, item 102590; *102:* quoted from the *Globe & Mail*, May 2, 1946; *104:* courtesy of Dorothy Powell; *106:* author's collection; *107:* CTA, SC 266, item 102591; *108:* Pier 21 Society; *110:* CTA, SC 266, item 102055; *110:* Pier 21 Society; *112:* Pier 21 Society; *114:* author's collection; *119:* courtesy of Jean Spear; *122, top:* courtesy of Jean Spear; *bottom:* NAC/ C-010371; *123 – 124:* Pier 21 Society; *126:* courtesy of the family of Johanna Taylor; *128:* Pier 21 Society; *131:* author's collection; *132:* Pier 21 Society; *133:* courtesy of Rosalind Walsh; *134:* author's collection; *135:* author's collection; *136:* Pier 21 Society; *back cover:* courtesy of Kay Garside.

Quotations from:
Canadian Cook Book for British Brides. Issued by Division of Women's Voluntary Services under the authority of The Hon. J. J. McCann, Minister of National War Services. 1945.
Canadian Soldier's Handbook of General Information. Issued by authority of the Minister of National Defence. 1943.
Welcome to War Brides. Published in Canada by the Department of National Defence and the Wartime Information Board. 1944.